IRAN

WHAT EVERYONE NEEDS TO KNOW®

IRAN

WHAT EVERYONE NEEDS TO KNOW®

MICHAEL AXWORTHY

OXFORD
UNIVERSITY PRESS

OXFORD
UNIVERSITY PRESS

Oxford University Press is a department of the University of Oxford. It furthers the University's objective of excellence in research, scholarship, and education by publishing worldwide. Oxford is a registered trade mark of Oxford University Press in the UK and certain other countries.

"What Everyone Needs to Know" is a registered trademark of Oxford University Press.

Published in the United States of America by Oxford University Press 198 Madison Avenue, New York, NY 10016, United States of America.

Library of Congress Cataloging-in-Publication Data
Names: Axworthy, Michael, author.
Title: Iran : what everyone needs to know / Michael Axworthy.
Description: New York, NY : Oxford University Press, 2017. |
Includes bibliographical references.
Identifiers: LCCN 2016034530 | ISBN 9780190232955 (hardback)
9780190232962 (paperback)
Subjects: LCSH: Iran—History—640– | Iran—Civilization.
Classification: LCC DS272 .A945 2017 | DDC 955—dc23
LC record available at https://lccn.loc.gov/2016034530

1 3 5 7 9 8 6 4 2

Paperback printed by LSC Communications, United States of America
Hardback printed by Bridgeport National Bindery, Inc.,
United States of America

For enlightenment of this kind, all that is needed is freedom. And the freedom in question is the most innocuous freedom of all—freedom to make public use of one's reason in all matters. But I hear on all sides the cry: Don't argue! The officer says: Don't argue, get on parade! The tax official: Don't argue, pay! The cleric: Don't argue, believe! . . . All this means restrictions on freedom everywhere. But which sort of restriction prevents enlightenment, and which, instead of hindering it, can actually promote it? I reply: The public use of man's reason must always be free, and it alone can bring about enlightenment among men . . .

—Immanuel Kant

Answering the Question:
What is Enlightenment?

CONTENTS

NOTE ON TRANSLITERATION

In this book, as in previous ones, I have sought to transliterate Persian words in a way that will sound familiar rather than alien to Iranians (hence Emam rather than Imam, Esmail rather than Ismail, and hejab rather than hijab, for example) and I have tried, and perhaps occasionally failed, to be consistent. There are also deliberate inconsistencies, notably over the transliteration of names that have had a life of their own in western writing: Isfahan, mullah, for example. Beyond that, in my view, there is scope for pedantry, but little for any claim to absolute correctness.

Michael Axworthy

IRAN

WHAT EVERYONE NEEDS TO KNOW®

INTRODUCTION

For many years, Iran has been closed off from much of the rest of the outside world, but now the country is opening up. The conclusion of the Joint Comprehensive Plan of Action (JCPOA) in July 2015 and the consequent implementation of commitments for the removal of sanctions on Iran in January 2016 have opened up a range of new opportunities—especially commercial opportunities—in relations between Iran and the rest of the world.

But it is never quite that simple. At the same time that these positive developments came to reality (developments that many, many skeptics had denied in previous months and years could ever come to pass), there were other, less welcome signs. In the autumn of 2015 Iran drew closer to Russia as both countries tried to shore up the Assad regime in Syria. At the beginning of 2016 relations between Iran and Saudi Arabia deteriorated after the Saudi authorities executed a prominent Shi'a cleric, and a Tehran mob sacked and partially burned the Saudi Embassy in response. In March 2016 Iran's Revolutionary Guard test-fired medium-range ballistic missiles in defiance of the concerns of the United States and others.

Why does Iran continue to show what appear to be such contradictory faces to the world? Why is the Iranian regime still so apparently determined not to fit in to the western idea of what a normal country should be? This book tries to answer those questions, and many others, through an explanation of Iranian history. The book has a historical structure, not just because the author is a historian, but because many of the big questions about Iranian attitudes and motivations in the present have deep historical roots. So for example, Iranian nationalism cannot be understood without reference to the nature and effects of the Arab conquest in the seventh century (and the other invasions of the following centuries). The version of political Islam expressed in the Islamic Republic cannot be understood without an explanation of the schism between Sunnism and Shi'ism that took place around the same time. Iranian attitudes to their neighbors in the Middle East draw largely upon the fact that their language is not Semitic but Indo-European in origin (like English)—to explain which it is necessary to go all the way back to the folk migrations of the second millennium BC. Iranian attitudes to the United States and United Kingdom were largely formed by the events of the imperial period in the nineteenth century, the two world wars in the twentieth, and the coup against Mohammad Mosaddeq in 1953.

A large part of the story of modern Iran is bound up in the rise of the clergy to a position of social leadership, their uncertainty about how to respond to the influence of the West in the country, their solution to that uncertainty in the form of Ruhollah Khomeini's grab for power in the revolution of 1979, and their trials and tribulations in securing and retaining that power since then.

An understanding of history is always useful, and sometimes indispensable, in attempting to understand predicaments in the present. This is all the more the case for Iran, whose history is so long, so complex, so important for Iranians, and so still relatively unknown for so many people in the rest of the world. This book, like the author's others, tries in a small way to help rectify that deficiency. The bibliography gives some guidance for further reading, but readers looking for greater detail, particularly about sources, should apply themselves to my previous books, especially *Revolutionary Iran* and *A History of Iran: Empire of the Mind* (published in the United Kingdom as *Iran: Empire of the Mind*).

Palazzo Pallavicini-Rospigliosi
Rome
October 2016

1

ANCIENT AND ISLAMIC IRAN

What do we know about the Indo-European peoples and the origins of Iran?

What we know begins with the fact that the Persian language (known to Iranians in their own tongue as Farsi) along with English and most other European languages, as well as Sanskrit, modern Hindi, and other languages of the Indian subcontinent, are all clearly and closely related in both grammar and vocabulary. So for example many basic words in Persian for people and relationships like *baradar* (brother), *dokhtar* (daughter, or girl), *madar* (mother), as well as others like *tondar* (thunder), *setareh* (star), *nam* (name), *mush* (mouse), *tarik* (dark), *dar* (door), and many more, are so close as often to be identical with the same words in English or other European languages. A few people had noticed this in earlier centuries, but the first serious scholar to do so, in 1786, was Sir William Jones, a judge working for the English East India Company (EIC). He and other employees of the EIC in India had to know Persian because Persian was the language of administration in Moghul India. With this supposition about the common origin of all these languages, Sir William founded the modern science of historical linguistics; he also produced many translations of Persian poetry and other texts.

Although the fact of the similarity of these languages is not disputed, it is almost the case to say that what we really know for sure about their similarity, and the origin of their similarity, ends with that observation too. Many theories to account for the similarity have been brought forward since Sir William's time. Most have assumed a common root and many scholars have accepted the idea of a pre-existing, now lost, proto-Indo-European language that was the common ancestor of all. Some have even traced back the earliest word and grammar forms to suggest what the outlines of that language could have been. At the same time, archaeologists and others have tried to identify where and when the people who spoke that language (or group of languages) may have lived. They *probably* came from somewhere in southern Russia, to the north of the Black and/or the Caspian seas, and some archaeologists have identified them as people who buried their dead in mound-tombs called kurgans in that region, in the period before around 2500 BC. At one time it was thought likely that the migration of peoples speaking ancient versions of German, Latin, Greek, Old Persian, and Sanskrit from that region into what are now Europe, Iran, and India was associated with the introduction of iron tools and weapons. Others have suggested that it was associated with the domestication of horses for the first time in that region.

All of this is speculative and far from certain. What is clearer is that between about 2500 BC and 1000 BC peoples speaking these languages moved from their original settlements into northern India, the Iranian plateau, Anatolia (if they were not already there by then), Greece, Italy, and central and northern Europe.

Scholars are also uncertain about the nature of the migration and settlement. In the nineteenth century, when crude nationalism infused thinking on these matters, the idea tended to be one of fire and sword: of folk movements en masse, with previous populations eradicated or forced to flee. In this crude model (which often, albeit unspoken, still underlies contemporary thinking on these subjects) blood and language were thought always to go together. Since then, it has been accepted that the reality must often have been more complex, and that even if violence was involved, it was often more about a small group settling, perhaps removing a previous elite ruling group, and asserting its dominance over a larger subject population, which then, over a long period, adopted the language and culture of the ruling group. It seems probable that the Iranian settlement followed a pattern more of this kind.

In Iran, archaeologists have found plentiful evidence of Stone Age and Bronze Age cultures predating the Indo-European/Iranian settlement. Some agricultural settlements that have been excavated in the Zagros Mountains go back as early as 8000 to 6000 BC, the period in which agriculture is first thought to have developed in this area. Different parts of the Tepe Sialk settlement near Kashan appear to have been occupied almost continuously from 5500 BC until well after 1000 BC. In southwestern Iran the Empire of Elam was an important and dynamic intermediary between the cultures of the Iranian plateau and Mesopotamia from around 4000 BC, when the city of Susa was founded.

It is likely that the incomers, speaking an Iranian language (or perhaps, even then, various Iranian dialects), probably nomadic or seminomadic pastoralists with a way of life based on cattle herding, inserted themselves into the preexisting pattern of settlement on the Iranian plateau in relatively small numbers initially (in the centuries before 1000 AD), asserting themselves over the previous inhabitants, and eventually assimilating with them. Iran has a radically varied climate and landscape, from lush subtropical forest in the north to harsh alpine, semi-arid,

arid, and desert conditions elsewhere, with large expanses of marsh, grassland, and other intermediate zones also. Along with some good agricultural land (especially in valleys and oases in the south and west, and in the north) there was a lot of marginal land suitable for seasonal grazing, which has always meant that large parts of Iran have been particularly adaptable for an extensive, migratory, nomadic pattern of land use by nomadic tribesmen. Such tribesmen always tend to have an uneasy relationship with neighboring settled populations; a relationship based partly on economic exchange (put crudely, grain and manufactured goods for wool and meat) but also on threat and protection—a security relationship arising from the fact that settled agriculturalists were always more vulnerable to raiding and the threat of raiding from the more mobile nomads than vice versa. In that security relationship (at least until the twentieth century) the nomadic tribes always tended to have the upper hand.

In the earliest evidence from Assyrian and Babylonian inscriptions (the very earliest is from 836 BC), the Iranian peoples appear as Medes, based in what is now northwestern Iran, and Persians, from the areas more to the south, associated with the sub-Elamite kingdom of Anshan. For centuries thereafter the Medes and Persians were the dominant peoples of the Iranian plateau.

How important was Zoroastrianism in Iranian and in world history?

Zoroastrianism today is a minority religion, with worshippers in India (especially in Bombay), a few in Iran, and smaller numbers scattered in the United States, Europe, Australia, and elsewhere in the world—probably less than 200,000 worldwide. But before the Islamic conquest of the seventh century, Zoroastrianism was the dominant religion of Iran. It had a profound influence on Judaism, Christianity, and Islam (the influence on the latter two was primarily indirect, through Judaism, but there were direct influences also). Even today, under the Islamic Republic, everyday life in Iran is marked by the ancient heritage of Zoroastrianism. The main festival of the year in Iran is still Now Ruz—new year—which falls on March 21, the spring equinox, as it did in the time of the ancient Iranian empires. The months of the year in the official calendar still carry the names of Zoroastrian subordinate deities or angels (*yazatas*) like Farvardin, Khordad, Tir, and Ordibehesht.

Modern scholarship has placed the origins of Zoroastrianism much earlier than the traditional date ascribed to it by the Zoroastrians themselves. Their view was that the religion originated with the prophet Zoroaster or Zarathustra (modern Persian *Zardosht*) in around 600 BC. But many (following the scholar Mary Boyce) now believe that Zoroaster, the founder of the religion, lived earlier— perhaps between 1500 BC and 1200 BC, or even earlier than that. It is problematic because the method of transmission for hundreds of years was primarily oral (as with early Sanskrit texts also) and the texts were probably not systematically recorded in written form until the Sassanid period (after 224 AD). But one reason for pushing the origins back earlier is that the language of the earliest Zoroastrian religious texts, the ones most closely associated with Zoroaster, is markedly different (closer to Sanskrit and proto-Indo-European) from later texts that can be identified with the political and cultural conditions around 600 BC. The language of those earliest texts (the *Gathas* of the *Avesta*) gives an impression of a world that can readily be identified with the nomadic, cattle-rearing way of life of the people who lived around the time of the original migration to the Iranian plateau.

Zoroaster's theology was organized around a stark, eternal conflict between Ahura Mazda, the creator-God of truth, light, and justice, and Ahriman, the embodiment of lies, darkness, injustice, and evil. This set up a strongly moral structure in which human freedom and choice were centrally important, stressing the importance of good thoughts, good words, and good actions. It also involved doctrines of judgment after death, and heaven and hell, that influenced Judaism and later religions. In particular, the terms for Truth and the Lie, *asha* and *druj*, recur insistently in the early Avestan texts, but they also appear frequently in surviving inscriptions and are echoed in Greek texts describing Iran or events in Iran.

Other (probably preexisting) deities were incorporated into the Zoroastrian religious structure as angels or archangels—notably Mithra, a sun god, and Anahita, a goddess of streams and rivers. Six immortal archangels (the *Amesha Spenta*) embodied animal life, plant life, metals and minerals, earth, fire, and water. The supreme deity, Ahura Mazda, personified air, and in origin probably paralleled the Greek Zeus, as a sky-god. The name Ahura Mazda means Lord of Wisdom, or Wise Lord. Because there seems to have been a large degree of diversity of belief in the early centuries after Zoroaster, encompassing similar but divergent religious traditions, and because the religion seems to have been more polytheistic than it later became (partly under pressure from Islam and Christianity), scholars have made a distinction between later Zoroastrianism and what they have called Mazdaism in the earlier period (the name reflecting the fact that all the different traditions include Ahura Mazda as a central figure).

In fourteenth-century England the Franciscan friar William of Occam came up with an important principle that has since been called Occam's Razor—that a scientific explanation which is simpler, and requires fewer new theoretical concepts, should always be preferred over one in which theoretical complications and new concepts proliferate. That principle has been important in scientific development since Occam's time—though today overlooked by some social scientists in fields like education. Pre-Islamic Mazdaism also followed the contrary path: it was characteristic of the religion that philosophical concepts or categories became personified as heavenly beings or entities—and over time these seem to have increased in number and multiplied. One example was the idea of the *daena*, which was held to appear in the form of a beautiful maiden to the soul of a just man after his death, being the personification of all the good works he had done in life. Elsewhere, and later, the word daena was used to signify religion itself—and it was carried over (in the form of the Arabic word *din*) with this meaning into Islam after the revelation of Mohammad. Another example of this proliferation in Mazdaism was the identification of *five* separate entities belonging to each human being—not just body, soul and spirit but also *adhvenak* and *fravashi*. Adhvenak was the heavenly prototype for each human being, associated with semen and regeneration. The fravashi, though also entities in the spirit world, were more active, associated with the strength of heroes, the protection of the living in life (like guardian angels), and the collection of souls after death (in this sense rather like the Valkyries in Germanic mythology). These and other personifications or angels prefigure the role of angels in Judaism, Christianity, and Islam, but also have parallels with the idea of forms in Platonism, and some scholars believe Plato was influenced by Mazdaism.

Another feature of Mazdaism that resurfaced later in Judaism, Christianity, and Islam was that of a Messiah. Within a few centuries, but at any rate before 600 BC, Mazdaism developed the idea of the Saoshyant, who would be born miraculously at the end of time from a virgin mother and the seed of Zoroaster himself. Like other religions (and other human institutions that mimic religions), Mazdaism was served by a priestly class, the Magi (listed by Herodotus as a distinct tribe among the Medes). The Magi survived from before the time of Zoroaster and interpreted and adapted doctrine and ritual to suit their own purposes, while remaining remarkably faithful to the central oral tradition. One symbol for the influence of Mazdaism on Christianity is the presence of the three Magi in the Gospel story of the birth of Jesus, effectively portraying a blessing of the new religion by the old.

Iranians and Jews have a long and complex history that often overlapped and interlocked in ancient times. Very early, after the conquest of the northern Kingdom of Israel by the Assyrians around 720 BC, large numbers of Jews were removed to Media, setting up long-lived Jewish communities, notably in Ecbatana/Hamadan. A second wave of deportations, this time to Babylonian territory, took place in the 590s and 580s BC, under Nebuchadnezzar, who destroyed the temple of Solomon in 586. Babylon came under Persian control in the 530s, and many of the Jews returned to Jerusalem thereafter. The Jews never forgot the trauma of the Babylonian exile nor the actions of the Achaemenid Persians in bringing it to a merciful end. One of the leaders of the return from Babylon, the scribe Ezra, is believed to have been the first to write down the books of the Torah (the first five books of the Bible, the books of Moses) in a new script. For hundreds of years after this, first under the Persian Empire and later under Hellenistic rulers, diaspora Jewish and Mazdaean religious communities lived adjacent to each other in cities all over what is now the Middle East. It is plain that many religious ideas became common currency, and the Qumran scrolls are just some of the sources that indicate a crossover of religious concepts from Mazdaism. There were later periods of strong influence too, in the second century BC and again in the fourth and fifth centuries AD, after the Roman destruction of Jerusalem. One of the strongest pointers to the persistent influence of Mazdaism is the generally positive attitude of the Jewish texts toward the Persians; a contrast with the hostile tendency in Greek classical writings.

The interpretation of Mazdaism and its development is complex and problematic. But heaven and hell, free human choice between good and evil, divine judgment, angels, a single creator-god, and a Messiah-like savior all appear to have been genuine early features of the religion, and were all hugely influential for religions that came later. It seems that Mazdaism was the first, in this part of the world at least, to move beyond cult and totemism to address moral and philosophical problems with its theology, from an individualistic standpoint that laid emphasis on personal choice and responsibility. Zoroaster can, in that sense, be said to have invented (or to have revealed) the modern moral world.

What was distinctive about the Achaemenid Empire, founded by Cyrus the Great in the sixth century BC?

In 549 BC a Persian, Cyrus, led a revolt that succeeded in capturing the capital of the Median Empire, Ecbatana (modern Hamadan). That event is the one usually taken as the date for the founding of the empire of the Achaemenid Persians (the dynasty was named after Cyrus's ancestor Achaemenes—a Greek version of the Persian name Hakhamenish). Where previously the Persians had been a subordinate people ruled by a Median dynasty, from 549 the situation was reversed. But from the beginning, the style of rule imposed by Cyrus seems to have been rather different, emphasizing a partnership between Medes and Persians (it seems likely that the Medes were more numerous, at least at first; and Cyrus may have had both Persian and Median lineage). In addition to the Medes and Persians, people associated with

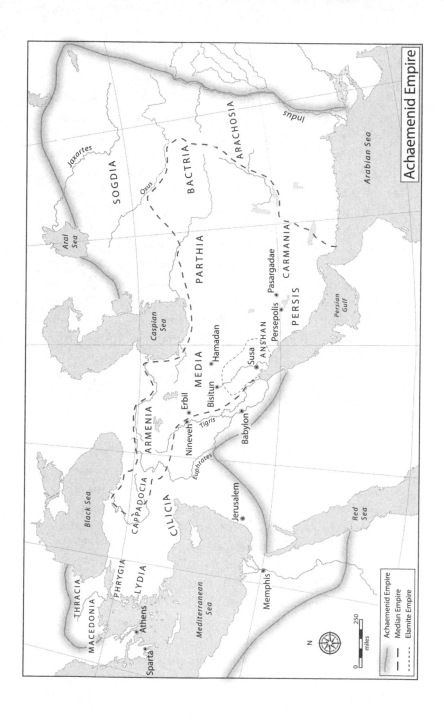

Achaemenid Empire

the earlier Elamite Empire seem to have had a continuing importance as bureaucrats and scribes—many of the Achaemenid court records were written in Elamite.

In later centuries Cyrus was celebrated as a model for wise, just kingship—notably in Xenophon's *Cyropedia*, and although that book was largely fictional, it does show the esteem in which he was held (despite the Greeks' habitual disdain for the Persians). The Jews were grateful to him for releasing them from captivity after his conquest of Babylon and for allowing them to return to rebuild their temple in Jerusalem. This picture is reinforced by the remarkable Cyrus cylinder, discovered in the ruins of Babylon in the nineteenth century and now held in the British Museum. Made and inscribed after Cyrus took Babylon in 539 (the city had revolted against its previous ruler), it does not celebrate with a list of captives, smitten enemies, and ruined cities, as do so many triumphal inscriptions from earlier Assyrian, Egyptian, and other empire builders. Cyrus chose instead to announce his clemency, generosity, and tolerance, deferring to the god of the Babylonians, Marduk—

> When I entered Babylon as a friend and when I established the seat of the government in the palace of the ruler under jubilation and rejoicing, Marduk, the great lord, induced the magnanimous inhabitants of Babylon to love me, and I was daily endeavouring to worship him. My numerous troops walked around in Babylon in peace, I did not allow anybody to terrorize any place of the country of Sumer and Akkad. I strove for peace in Babylon and in all his other sacred cities. . .

It seems that Cyrus allowed all his subject peoples, not just the Babylonians and the Jews, to worship their own gods. In his time and later, they were also ruled with their own customs and laws, often by rulers (satraps) descended from local dynasties. Not all his successors followed his example as closely as they might have, but in general Persian rule had a loose, devolved style. It is notable that Cyrus and his successors did not seek to impose their own, Mazdaean religion; but it is not fanciful to see the moral character of that religion and its emphasis on truth, integrity, and justice emerging in this new, firm, but tolerant style of rule. Those qualities reemerge in inscriptions of a later Achaemenid, Darius I, at Bisitun and the great palace of Persepolis (built from about 515 BC). Recent scholarship has thrown doubt on Darius's own claim to integrity and truthfulness, but his propaganda nevertheless underscores the qualities that were thought of by contemporaries to characterize just rule, even if the reality of his conduct fell somewhat short. The Achaemenid Empire was founded and confirmed not just as an empire of the sword, but as an empire based on an idea—an Empire of the Mind.

By the end of his reign Cyrus had conquered a larger empire than any the world had seen up to that time, from the Aegean to the Indus valley; his son Cambyses extended it further by adding Egypt. Darius I went further again, conquering Thrace and Macedon and initiating a series of wars between Persian and Greek that left a deep and lasting mark on the way that later Europeans viewed Persia, and the Orient generally. Overlooking their own brutalities and other failings, the Greeks (especially the Athenians) tended to caricature the Persians as decadent, tyrannical, and cruel: generalizations that were never wholly justified, if at all. As we have already seen, the biblical account of the Achaemenids is a valuable corrective.

Greek prejudice against the Achaemenids is a reminder of something else; that the history of the Achaemenids, whether from Greek classical texts or from inscriptions transcribed in the nineteenth century, has come to us (and to modern Iranians) through western writing and scholarship, not through an Iranian historical tradition. The use of the term "Persia" also reflects this. Because the Achaemenids came from the province of Persis, the Greeks called them and other inhabitants of their empire Persians. Following this precedent (as in so many other ways) the Romans called peoples from this same region Persians too, in their time; and Europeans later, educated largely from the Greek and Roman classics, did so as well, all the way through until the nineteenth century (absorbing many of the Greek and Roman prejudices about the Persians along the way). But all through these long eras Iranians called their country "Iran." Finally, in 1935 Reza Shah Pahlavi formally asked all foreign embassies in his country to call the country Iran in official communications (partly for nationalist reasons and partly to distinguish his own rule from that of the Qajar dynasty that he had ousted), and Iran has been the name in general usage since that time. Notwithstanding all that, Iranians still today call their language "Farsi"—Persian— because in pre-Islamic Iran the dialect of Fars province (ancient Pars or Persis) became, and remained later, the culturally dominant one.

How did monarchy and government change in the Parthian and Sassanid periods (c. 250 BC to 642 AD)?

The course of Iranian history is marked by several major external interruptions. The first of these was the invasion of Alexander the Great from 334 BC, which brought the Achaemenid dynasty and its empire to an end. Alexander's own style of rule, once he had consolidated his grip over the Iranian plateau, was relatively relaxed, along similar lines to that of Cyrus. He was an autocrat (there was no suggestion of any Athenian-style democracy) but he showed respect to the conquered Persians, and tried to bring about a fusion of Greek and Persian cultures, encouraging intermarriage. After Alexander's death in Babylon in 323 BC, his

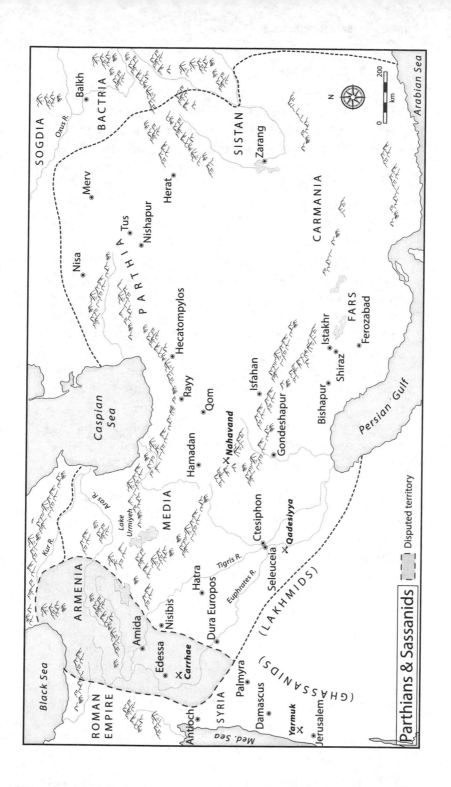

Parthians & Sassanids

⌐ ⌐ ⌐ Disputed territory

Arabian Sea

SOGDIA

BACTRIA

Balkh

Oxus R.

SISTAN

Zarang

200

N

km

0

Merv

Herat

CARMANIA

PARTHIA

Tus

Nishapur

Nisa

Hecatompylos

FARS

Istakhr

Ferozabad

Rayy

Isfahan

Shiraz

Caspian Sea

Qom

Bishapur

Nahavand

Gondeshapur

Persian Gulf

Hamadan

MEDIA

Aras R.

Lake Urmiyeh

Ctesiphon

Qadesiyya

Kur R.

Tigris R.

Seleucia

Hatra

Euphrates R.

ARMENIA

Dura Europos

(LAKHMIDS)

Amida

Nisibis

Black Sea

Edessa

Carrhae

ROMAN EMPIRE

Palmyra

(GHASSANIDS)

SYRIA

Antioch

Damascus

Yarmuk

Med. Sea

Jerusalem

empire was divided between his generals, and the eastern part was taken over by Seleucus Nicator (after a series of wars in which less fortunate officers were eliminated and their territories absorbed by others). Seleucus continued the precedent set by his former master, favoring a partnership with his Persian subjects and a devolved style of rule, but he and his successors were for the most part looking westward, trying to achieve the conquest of Egypt, Asia Minor, Greece, and the full extent of Alexander's empire. They had some successes but never fully succeeded. Instead several of their territories in the east revolted and made themselves independent. One of these was Parthia (roughly in the territory of present-day Turkmenistan and the northern part of the Iranian province of Khorasan), the home of a people who still followed an older pattern of Iranian nomadic life.

The Parthians' culture revolved around horses, and their armies were almost wholly composed of horse-archers, with a smaller number of armored lancers. Between 250 BC and 80 BC, with some setbacks, they spread into the eastern provinces of the Seleucid Empire, which was gradually squeezed out of existence between them and the Romans, who were expanding eastward. The early period of their expansion in the northeast was associated both with Greeks rebelling against the Seleucids (including the founders of the state of Bactria, even further east) and with the beginnings of the hugely profitable trade along the Silk Road. It seems probable that the value of this trade route, running through a region where many Greeks had settled in new cities, explains at least in part why the early Parthian kings laid great emphasis on their friendliness with the Greeks—stating that with the word *philhellenon* on their coinage, for example, which was inscribed with Greek lettering and followed Greek patterns of design. Like the Seleucids and Achaemenids, they governed at arms' length, through regional princes or satraps.

After the Seleucid state had been extinguished, the Parthians came into direct confrontation with the Romans in Syria and eastern Anatolia. In 53 BC an invading army led by the Roman statesman Marcus Licinius Crassus was defeated by a smaller Parthian force at the battle of Carrhae, in what is now eastern Turkey. It was one of the most humiliating defeats ever suffered by the Romans and was never forgotten, prompting later Roman generals and emperors to try to succeed where Crassus had failed. Initially, few did—until the emperor Trajan made use of the Tigris and Euphrates rivers to campaign against the Parthians successfully in Mesopotamia and capture the Parthian capital Ctesiphon in 116 AD, taking the title "Parthicus" in recognition of his triumph. For both the Parthians and the Romans, the wars were partly about the possession of valuable territories in northern Mesopotamia, Syria, and Armenia. But they were also, perhaps more importantly, about prestige. Ctesiphon was captured only briefly, and Trajan's successor Hadrian abandoned his eastern conquests, but the Romans took and sacked Ctesiphon twice again in the next eighty years—in 164 and 197.

These repeated crises probably contributed to the collapse of the Parthian monarchy a few years later, in 224 AD. The last Parthian king, Artabanus IV, was defeated in battle and replaced as king by the head of a new dynasty, the Sassanids, who called himself Ardashir. Rather than emphasizing Greek connections, Ardashir and his successors stressed their Iranian, Persian, and Mazdaean identity. The name Ardashir itself harked back to the name of more than one important Achaemenid king—Artaxerxes, and the Sassanids came from Fars province, like the Achaemenids. They enjoyed a closer relationship with the clergy, and some of Ardashir's own ancestors had been priests. As if to prove to the world that they and not the Parthians had been the rightful rulers, Ardashir and his successor Shapur achieved a series of victories over the Romans in the decades after 224 AD, culminating in 260 AD with Shapur's capture of the Roman emperor Valerian.

The balance of fortunes in the seemingly interminable series of wars see-sawed back and forth, but in the mid-fifth century the Romans and Persians made a kind of truce because they both faced a new threat from the north—from the Huns. The Sassanid Empire nearly went under—it survived partly because the Huns moved west to attack the western Roman Empire. But the Huns were just one aspect of a more general crisis at this time—famine, disease, and the effects of excessive taxation all seem to have added to the pressure. The sources for this period are sparse and were written down much later, but it appears that the crisis produced a kind of communist revolt, led by a Zoroastrian heretic prophet, Mazdak, who preached that since private property and the desire for women caused all the evil in the world, the solution must be to hold all property and women in common (so long as the women consented, and it seems quite a few did). The king seems for a time to have allied himself with Mazdak's revolt, using it to humble the nobility and clergy, who had become over-mighty and arrogant in the preceding period. When this process was complete, the king rejected Mazdak and convened a kind of tribunal of other religious leaders (Zoroastrian, Christian, and Jewish) to condemn him. Then Mazdak and his followers were put to death. But the episode had created a new social and political settlement, in which the king acted as an arbitrator and guarantor between the different social classes, keeping them in balance and ensuring justice. Some have pointed to the similarity of these arrangements to the shape of politics later, in medieval Europe. The kings also enhanced the social position of the gentry (dehqans), which had the effect of strengthening the army and the monarchy.

This new model of kingship reached its apogee under Khosraw I Anushirvan, who reigned from 531 to 579 AD. Khosraw was famous in later ages for his just and wise rule. He was successful in war, but also encouraged learning and science, organizing the collection and translation of texts from all over the known world. His reign was later (after the Islamic conquest) looked back on as a Golden Age, and Sassanid government took its final form under him. According to this theory of government, success in war showed the favor of God and gave the king an aura of royal glory (*kvarr* or later *farr*) that showed he had the right to rule. But this right was conditional, not absolute—if the king ruled justly, his subjects would be prosperous and supportive, taxation would be plentiful and his armies strong, defending the empire and the king's own right successfully—a virtuous circle. But if unjust, the subjects would become mutinous and poor, taxation would dwindle, the armies would become weak, and the king would lose his *farr*—a vicious circle. He would also lose his battles, and God would give his favor to a usurper. The key was justice and just rule. This theoretical structure of government, postulated (if never fully achieved) in the last flowering of the Sassanid Empire, was reinterpreted later, after the Arab conquest (especially in the period of the Abbasid caliphate, after 750 AD), was readopted, and dominated ideas about government over the whole Islamic world for centuries.

In the early years of the seventh century the Sassanids renewed war with the eastern Roman Empire (usually called the Byzantine Empire by this later period) and achieved dramatic successes, extending briefly almost to the ancient Achaemenid boundaries. But within a short time the Byzantines fought back, penetrating to the heart of Sassanid territory and inflicting a defeat (at Nineveh in 627) that wiped out all the Persians' previous victories. The wars were damaging to both sides through the action of the armies, but also through disruption of trade, creation of famine, the spread of disease, and the permanent loss of agricultural land through the abandonment or destruction of vital irrigation works. This weakening of the Sassanid and Byzantine empires is thought greatly to have helped the rapid expansion of Muslim conquests after the death of the Prophet in 632 AD, the next great interruption in Iranian history.

Why was the Muslim conquest of Iran so rapid, and why was there a schism between Sunni and Shi'a?

One reason for the rapid expansion of the Islamic empire was the exhaustion of the neighboring empires after the previous wars, but the other major reason was the cohesion and determination given to the Arab Muslim forces by their new religious faith. The early history of Islam is important for Iran because it explains the history of how Iran became Muslim, but also because it explains the origins of Shi'ism, the faith of most Iranians today.

The Prophet Mohammad began to preach the revelation of Islam in Mecca from about 613 AD. Encountering opposition and hostility there, in 622 he moved with his followers to Medina, where he became accepted as the leader of the community and converted the inhabitants to the new religion. War with Mecca was concluded successfully when the Meccans submitted in 630, and by the time of Mohammad's death in 632 a large part of the peoples of the Arabian peninsula had been converted. After his death there were divisions among his followers, and Abu Bakr, who took over leadership of the Muslims as caliph, used raiding and warfare against neighboring unbelievers to encourage unity. There was also an impetus to spread the new religion and make new converts, but the rapid success of Islamic expansion may have surprised even the Arabs. Within just twenty years they had decisively defeated the Byzantines and the Persians, conquering Egypt, Palestine, Syria, and all the central territories of the former Sassanid Empire. The Byzantines managed to hold on to most of Anatolia, and their western provinces, until the eleventh century; but the Sassanid dynasty and its empire were destroyed. Zoroastrianism was eclipsed and began its slow decline to become a minority religion. Muslims did not convert by force as a rule, but over centuries the advantages of conversion to the ruling faith had their inevitable effect. For hundreds of years thereafter, Iranians were mainly ruled by princes and dynasties of foreign origin.

The conquests and the euphoria of their achievement did sustain a sense of common purpose among the Arabs. But there were serious divisions within the community of Muslims (the *umma*) nonetheless—and the consequences of the conquests and the riches they yielded created further problems. In the history of Christianity, the major schisms between Orthodox and Catholic, and later between Catholic and Protestant, only developed after many centuries and were largely about theology. The main schism in Islam by contrast, between Sunni and Shi'a, goes right back to the death of the prophet in 632 AD, and centered on the question of leadership.

When Mohammad died, a significant group of his followers believed that his son-in-law, Ali, should have become caliph instead of Abu Bakr. This group later became known as the *Shi'a Ali*—the party of Ali. Ali did eventually become caliph, after the death of Abu Bakr and two successors, but his caliphate was troubled. Ali was assassinated in 661 AD by a member of another group, the Kharijites, who felt he had betrayed them by compromising too easily with his opponents, who were led by Mu'awiya, the governor of Syria. After Ali's death Mu'awiya became caliph, the first of the Umayyad dynasty. The Shi'a (the term did not really come into use until later, but it is convenient to use it for this earlier period too) believed that the caliphate should have gone to Ali's descendants (who were, of course, Mohammad's descendants also), not to Mu'awiya and the Umayyads.

Within a short time the Umayyads acquired a reputation for luxury and immorality, fueled by the huge wealth of the conquests. In 680, encouraged by the people of Kufa in Iraq, Ali's son Hosein (the Prophet's grandson) rebelled against the Umayyad caliph Yazid and took a small group of followers toward Kufa. Before they got there, troops sent by Yazid intercepted Hosein at Karbala and after he refused to surrender, massacred him and most of his people, capturing the rest. This was a huge event in the history of Islam; the Shi'a in particular have never forgotten it and commemorate it with processions each year at the Ashura anniversary. The division between the Shi'a and the majority Sunni Muslims (the term Sunni denotes the followers of *sunna*—the traditions of the sayings and actions of the Prophet) was entrenched and embittered by the massacre of Karbala, and has remained so ever since. The Shi'a have always been a minority (today they number no more than 15 percent of the world population of Muslims) and have often been persecuted: though there have been episodes when Shi'a rulers took power—notably the Fatimids in Egypt and North Africa between the tenth and the twelfth centuries. Many Sunni Muslims (not just the most extreme) regard the Shi'a as heretics, believing in particular that their veneration of Ali, Hosein, and their descendants (the Shi'a Emams) is idolatrous and unacceptably polytheistic.

The main centers of Shi'a pilgrimage have always been the shrine cities of Najaf (where Ali lies buried) and Karbala, both in what is now Iraq, and until the sixteenth century Iran was not a predominantly Shi'a territory. But the Safavid dynasty that took power there in 1501 made Shi'ism the state religion, and since then Iran has been the preeminent state of Shi'a Islam. Iranian Shi'as are twelver Shi'as, which means they venerate the succession of Emams up to the twelfth, who they believe disappeared in the mid-ninth century. They believe the twelfth Emam did not die but will return at the end of the world (with Jesus at his shoulder). Other smaller Shi'a sects (notably the Ismailis) have different beliefs about the succession of Emams (where Shi'as are mentioned elsewhere in this book, it is normally twelver Shi'ism that is meant). The schism between Sunni and Shi'a has always been important, but has grown in importance in the early years of the twenty-first century with the rise of political Islam, of extremist Sunni sects like the Wahhabis and Salafis (usually strongly hostile to Shi'as), and the regional rivalry between Iran and Saudi Arabia.

What was Sufism and why was it so important in medieval Iran?

In simple terms, Sufism is the main mystical tradition in Islam, which emphasizes personal spiritual experience and an attempt to reach a direct contact with God through meditation, prayer, and other means.

But Sufism has been much more significant than those bare facts would suggest. Sufis were important in Iran and beyond in the medieval period because they made most of the conversions in the countryside, remoter areas, and new territories (Anatolia and northern India, for example). The missionary function of spreading Islam fell to them because their chosen way of life tended to emphasize humility, poverty, and association with the humbler classes of the population, including nomadic peoples, while the religious scholars, the *ulema*, tended to stay in the towns and cities, where the mosques and books were to be found. Tending to be somewhat in opposition to the legalistic tradition of the ulema, the Sufis were hugely influential more widely in Iranian life, especially in literature but also in music and in other ways.

Whereas the shari'a tradition in Islam grew up out of the need to interpret the Qoran and the traditions (hadith) about the sayings and actions of the Prophet, one can see Sufism as originating in an attempt by spiritually inclined people to experience themselves the kind of direct contact with God that Mohammad experienced, and which produced the revelation of the Qoran. Another way of understanding the Sufi phenomenon is as a reaction against the shari'a tradition of the ulema—rejecting the idea that a religious life was just about following established rituals and rules of conduct. This rejection could be quite extreme—Sufi poetry often celebrated the wild, outcast *rend* or *qalandar*, who wear rags, drink wine, dance ecstatically, roam the world begging for their food, associate with non-Muslims, and enjoy sexual liaisons outside marriage. One aspect of this extreme behavior was simple defiance of the puritanical religious scholars and their rules; another was that the Sufis believed that the highest religious experience could only be attained by immolation of the Ego. One route to this was through asceticism, poverty and the abandonment of social or other ambitions, but drunkenness and sexual love were also celebrated as metaphors (at least) for the loss of the sense of Self. Another, more concealed aspect was the continuing influence of pre-Islamic traditions—notably the sub-Zoroastrian movement of the communist Mazdakites of the fifth century and the later Khorramites of the eighth and ninth centuries; but also neo-Platonism and Christian Gnosticism (an additional pointer in this direction is the proliferation of categories in Sufi philosophy). Post-Islamic Iran was a place where many wildly eclectic religious and political movements bubbled to the surface, and the association with later Sufism is obvious. Most of the Sufi orders were Sunni-inclined, but their unconventional and rebellious inclinations also made an affinity with Shi'ism.

Of the great Persian poets, Rumi was an avowed Sufi and founded a Sufi order in the thirteenth century that still exists today, based in Konya in Turkey. Others like Sanai and Attar were also Sufis; Hafez is less explicitly Sufi but like most of the other poets his language is infused by Sufi images, concepts, and usages—similarly with Sa'di and Omar Khayyam.

Through their missionary activities, their literary influence, and in other ways the Sufis had a huge and enduring effect on the Islamic world—and perhaps beyond. Some have noted thought-provoking similarities between Sufi beliefs and practices, and those of troubadours and Franciscan friars in Europe in the Middle Ages—perhaps especially those of Saint Francis of Assisi himself.

How did Iran survive the many invasions during the centuries that followed the Islamic conquest, and what real continuity was there between pre-Islamic and post-Islamic Iran?

After the Arab conquest of the seventh century, Iran was invaded by the Seljuk Turks in the eleventh century, by the Mongols in the thirteenth century, and by Timur (Tamerlane) and a new wave of Turco-Mongol warrior-nomads at the end of the fourteenth. Through all these centuries, the territory of Iran was ruled by non-Iranians for the most part. All of the invasions were damaging and disruptive at least, and some of them were devastating. The Mongol invasions of 1220–1221, initially given extra punitive ferocity by Ghengis Khan's anger at the mistreatment of his ambassadors, destroyed several great

Iranian cities in what are now Afghanistan, Tajikistan, and Turkmenistan as well as Iranian Khorasan. These eastern cities had been enriched by the silk trade and often by extensive (and high-maintenance) agricultural irrigation works in their hinterland. Many of them (Nishapur, Tus, Balkh) had been the homes of famous poets and centers of Sufism. The region of Khorasan as a whole (in medieval times encompassing all this territory) had been the prime center for a process in which Arab and Persian cultures had mingled and fused, producing a Golden Age for the Persian language, literature, and science. In several of the cities (Merv, Urgench, and Balkh for example), previously large urban centers with populations of several hundred thousand, the Mongols and their Turkish auxiliaries massacred or abducted almost the whole population. Irrigation works were destroyed or fell into disuse and large tracts of previously productive arable land were given over to pasture for sheep, goats, and horses. Some of the cities were rebuilt or partially rebuilt, only to be devastated again by Timur in 1383–1385. The Mongol invasions effectively ended the great flowering of Islamic Iranian civilization that had followed the Islamic conquest in Khorasan.

But within a couple of generations the Mongol conquerors had converted to Islam and their rulers' courts were full of Persian-speaking Iranians. As before with the Seljuks and Arabs, the Iranians proved themselves indispensable as scribes and bureaucrats for the administration of new dynasties and empires. With the scribes and bureaucrats came poets, clerics, manuscript illustrators, architects, and craftsmen of all kinds; all indispensable to the sort of court that the Iranian courtiers convinced the conquerors, over time, that they needed. Persian civilization was not snuffed out; it adapted and shifted location. Within a few years of Timur's irruption, a new Timurid court at Herat was presiding over another great flowering of Persianate culture, under the rule of his son Shahrokh.

This ability to reassert cultural influence—indeed cultural dominance—over successive waves of foreign conquerors was one aspect of the survival of Iranian language and culture in the centuries after the Islamic conquest. But it also says something important about the high level of sophistication and self-confidence that Sassanid court culture had attained in the last centuries before the Arabs came, and the resilience of some social classes—especially the *dehqan* class, the gentry who had provided the cavalry of the Sassanid army and who had benefited from the reforms of the monarchy in its penultimate phase.

The crucial element in the question of continuity through this period is the Persian language. One way to look at it is to say that Persian changed, adapted, simplified, and reemerged after the Islamic conquest in a new form. Another way to look at it is to say that a new language was created through the impact of Arabic and Islam on the preexisting Persian language forms. Modern Persian is less grammatically complex than the Middle Persian of the Sassanid period, and it contains a large proportion of words taken from Arabic. There are some parallels with the way that modern English emerged at the end of the Middle Ages, having absorbed many loanwords from French, the language of the ruling class of Norman conquerors. Just as, later, Shakespeare appeared in the early decades after modern English emerged in its fresh, new form, so the greatest Persian poets appeared in the decades and centuries following the emergence of modern Persian—as if the new possibilities offered by the new language form had in themselves stimulated new, more sophisticated, subtle and beautiful forms of expression.

One of the earliest of these poets was Ferdowsi, whose great work the *Shahnameh* deliberately celebrated pre-Islamic Iran: its religion, martial culture, and above all its monarchy. In doing so Ferdowsi deliberately used language that to a large extent avoided the use of the Arabic words that had become common in Persian by his time. His work seems to have built on writings that survived from the Sassanid period and the work of the earlier poet Daqiqi. Both Daqiqi and Ferdowsi had benefited from the patronage of the Samanid court, based in the city of Balkh in what is now Afghanistan; the Samanids had used Persian as the language of their court and had deliberately encouraged the celebration of Persian culture and traditions as a matter of policy.

Along with Hafez, who lived later, Ferdowsi is probably the poet whose work has been most familiar to ordinary Iranians in modern times. The stories in his great poem, of Sohrab and Rostam, Khosrow and Shirin, Bijan and Manijeh, and many others, are familiar to Iranians today as they have been for centuries; and sayings and phrases from the stories are often quoted. With the other, later poets, Ferdowsi helped to fix and stabilize the Persian language in a comparable way to Shakespeare and the King James Bible in English or Luther's Bible in German, or Dante's *Inferno* in Italian; cementing at the same time a sense of Iranian identity.

It is plain that the Arab conquest marked a major break in Iranian history, deepened by the trauma of the later invasions. But it is clear also that the Samanids, and Ferdowsi, and many of the Persian courtiers under the Abbasids and later rulers, felt a strong need to maintain a continuity from the court and intellectual culture of Sassanid Iran, and despite harsh and unpromising circumstances, were largely successful. Not just that—on the basis of that inheritance they helped to bring about a new flowering of Persianate culture that far surpassed anything that had gone before.

Who were the great thinkers and poets of medieval Iran?

In writing about the contribution of Iranians to Islamic culture, there is a danger of being thought partisan. Perhaps with that in mind, the scholar Richard Frye, in his classic account of what he called the Golden Age of Persia, quoted the great Arab thinker Ibn Khaldun, who wrote in the fourteenth century that most of the great scholars of religious law, of the intellectual sciences, and even the grammarians of the Arabic language itself had been non-Arabs—they had been Persians who had learned Arabic. "Only the Persians engaged in the task of preserving knowledge and writing systematic scholarly works." Ibn Khaldun in turn quoted the Prophet himself as having said "If learning were suspended at the highest parts of heaven the Persians would attain it." One should not overstate it, and there were of course many important scholars and thinkers from other parts of the Islamic world, but the Persian contribution to the flowering of Islamic culture in the eighth to the thirteenth centuries was enormous.

The crucial development was the establishment of the Abbasid caliphate at the new city of Baghdad after the successful Abbasid revolt of the mid-eighth century. Where the previous Umayyad dynasty had originated from a power base in Syria and had been marked by Byzantine influences, the Abbasid revolt had begun in Khorasan and from the beginning had a pronounced Persianate character. In the decades and centuries that followed most of the court scribes and bureaucrats were Persians, even though they had learned Arabic in order to conduct business. When the Abbasid caliphs established centers of learning (most notably the Beit al-Hikma founded by caliph Harun al-Rashid in Baghdad around the year 800 AD and augmented by his son al-Mamun later) they followed Sassanid models, just as they had followed Khosrow Anushirvan in their ideas about court life and the conduct of government. Later dynasties and their courts (like the Samanids and others) in turn emulated the Abbasids, in their patronage of learning and literature as in government. The result was an explosion of intellectual activity—in areas related to religious studies like speculative theology, philosophy, mysticism, religious law, grammar and linguistic study, and the translation of works from other languages but also, often stimulated by the translations, in areas like mathematics (al-Khwarazmi, al-Buzjani, Omar Khayyam), medicine (al-Sarakhsi, al-Razi, ibn Sina), astronomy (al-Fazari, al-Nihavandi, al-Farghani, Nasir al-Din Tusi), history (al-Tabari), and the theory of government (many, but notably Nizam ol-Mulk). Many important figures were polymaths with wide interests, like the Musa brothers and al-Biruni, who were important in both mathematics and astronomy, and Ibn Sina, who wrote on medicine, logic, astronomy, and many other subjects. Many of their names became known in the west (albeit often in garbled form) as western learning itself expanded in the twelfth century, stimulated by the expansion of monastic endowments, the establishment of the first universities, and the translation of new texts passed on through the Islamic world—most notably, the works of Aristotle. Thus Ibn Sina was known in the west as Avicenna and al-Farghani as Alfraganus, for example.

The works of these thinkers and scientists went well beyond mere copying from earlier authorities or commentaries; they made many new discoveries in astronomy, medicine, and mathematics in particular. So for example, al-Razi (thought to have been born around 850 AD and died in 925) was the first to differentiate between smallpox and measles as separate diseases. He emphasized the necessity for observation and critical thinking—establishing, in effect, some of the fundamental features of what we would call scientific method—and wrote a book setting out short-comings and errors he had found in the writings of the great Greek medical authority Galen. He also acquired a reputation for skepticism about religion (as did Omar Khayyam later). Al-Biruni (born 973) contributed to some of the same thinking on medicine and scientific method, and wrote also on comparative religion, producing a book on the religion, customs, geography, and history of India that was a model of objectivity and tolerance. Ibn Sina was born around 980 AD; his *Canon of Medicine* was translated into Latin in the thirteenth century and later into many other European languages, and was the standard medical textbook in Europe until it began to be superseded in the latter part of the seventeenth century. His philosophical works were also influential.

Again, the great intellectual outpouring of the ninth to the thirteenth centuries was not just a Persian phenomenon. There were many great thinkers and scientists from other parts of the Islamic world also. But the Persian contribution was unparalleled.

Drawing partly on the intellectual surge that followed the establishment of the Abbasid caliphate, on the later development of Persianate regional courts like that of the Samanids, on the continuing cultural ferment in Khorasan, on the new opportunities for expression offered by new language forms, and perhaps above all on the parallel growth of the Sufi movement, Persian poetry evolved in this period into something new, sophisticated, and unprecedented. It is difficult to give a proper sense of this in a short space. The sheer quantity of poetry produced by the best poets is daunting in itself. We have already mentioned Ferdowsi (a contemporary of Ibn Sina); a younger contemporary was Naser-e Khosraw (born in 1003), who wrote around 30,000 lines of poetry, of which about 11,000 have survived. His work, like that of many who came after him, was more philosophical and religious in character than that of Ferdowsi.

Omar Khayyam (born around 1048) is best known in the west for his poetry, largely (in the English-speaking world) through the free translations or reinterpretations of Edward Fitzgerald, which became hugely popular at the end of the nineteenth century. But in the eastern tradition and in Iran, Khayyam is famous mainly as a mathematician and a scientist, being credited inter alia with arguing for the heliocentric model of the solar system (though many others have been claimed as the first to do so) and devising an accurate calendar. In fact, relatively little poetry can be definitively attributed to him. Most of it is in the four-line ruba'i form—but a larger quantity was ascribed to him in later centuries, seemingly because other poets imitating his skeptical voice let their work go under his name to avoid censure from the religious authorities. So for example—

Good and evil, which are in the nature of mankind,
Joy and sadness, which are in fate and destiny;
Do not attribute them to the wheeling machinery of the heavens.
That wheel is a thousand times more helpless than you.

Reflecting the strength of the movement in Khorasan and elsewhere at that time, most of the notable poets of the twelfth century were Sufis. There were many, but three of the most important were Sanai, Nizami Ganjavi, and Farid al-Din Attar (born around 1158). Attar is believed to have penned over 45,000 lines in his lifetime; he died in Nishapur when that city was destroyed during the Mongol invasions of the 1220s. He became famous above all for his beautiful long poem *The Conference of the Birds*—itself an extended allegory for the Sufi's mystical journey toward spiritual fulfillment, and one of the greatest expressions of Sufism as the religion of love.

Perhaps the greatest Sufi poet of all, Jalal al-Din Molavi Rumi, was born near Balkh a few years before the Mongols arrived. But fortunately his father moved away ahead of the Mongols, eventually settling in Konya in what is now Turkey. Rumi's greatest poem, the *Masnavi*, begins—

> *Now listen to this reed-flute's deep lament*
> *About the heartache being apart has meant*

—establishing the metaphor of longing for reunion with the Beloved (and with God), explored by Rumi and his many followers and successors. The Molavi order of Sufis founded by his followers in his memory still commemorates him in Konya, where he is buried. In recent years Rumi has become more popular again in translation, especially in the United States.

Fakhroddin 'Iraqi was perhaps the poet who most embodied the Sufi archetype of the antinomian *rend* or *qalandar*, rejecting religious and social convention. He took this path when still in his teens; having been a devoted scholar in his home city of Hamadan, his head was turned when some *qalandari* Sufis arrived there, and he left with them, never to return. 'Iraqi was a follower of the great Sufi thinker Ibn 'Arabi, and he was buried next to Ibn 'Arabi in Damascus when he died in 1289.

Sa'di and Hafez, while influenced by Sufism, may not have been committed Sufis themselves. Both were born in Shiraz and, like Ferdowsi, are so well known to ordinary Iranians that phrases from their poetry have become part of everyday speech. Many of Sa'di's poems tell stories, and have a proverbial quality that lends itself to quotation. Many Iranians would say that Hafez (born around 1315) was the greatest poet of all. For centuries they have used his *divan* (the book of his collected poems) for what is called *fal*, a kind of divination, by opening it at random and interpreting the lines on the chosen page for insight into the future.

There have been many more poets in Persian since the fourteenth century but these, who lived before that time, have had by common consensus a huge effect on Iranian culture and thinking. Some, like the twentieth-century historian Ahmad Kasravi, have criticized the poetic tradition for contributing to a certain disposition to ambiguity and evasiveness of mind among Iranians—for enabling people to deal with an awkward question with a pithy and familiar quotation rather than a direct answer or deeper thought. But few dispute the beauty and value of the poetry. It is one of the greatest contributions that Iran has made to human civilization.

2

THE SAFAVIDS AND
THE IMPACT OF
THE WEST (1500–1921)

When and why did Iran turn Shi'a?

At the beginning of the sixteenth century a new empire was established on the Iranian plateau—the empire of the Safavids. The Safavid dynasty originated in Ardebil and the surrounding area, in the eastern part of what is now the northwestern Iranian province of Azerbaijan, in the turmoil that followed on from the Mongol invasions of the thirteenth century. It was founded by Sheikh Safi (1252–1334), who gave the dynasty its name. The Safavids were the leaders of a Sufi brotherhood, but in the fourteenth and fifteenth centuries they expanded their influence and connections among the militant Turkic tribes and clans in Azerbaijan and eastern Anatolia through strategic marriage alliances and charismatic leadership.

In the fifteenth century, under the leadership of Sheikh Junayd (1447–1460), the Safavids and their followers allied themselves with the Aq-Qoyunlu (the White Sheep Turks)—then the dominant power in the ancient territories of Iran. The Safavids made successful raids into Christian Georgian territory and developed into a significant military force, later fighting other local Muslim tribal groups. Their military strength was based on the Qezelbash: highly motivated, aggressive horsemen fired with religious devotion and personal attachment to their Safavid sheikh. Having been Sunni originally, the Safavids had expanded their following to include many tribal adherents with a strong attachment to the Emam Ali, turning increasingly Shi'a (albeit at a low theological level: the level of enthusiastic but illiterate folk belief). At the beginning of the sixteenth century their young leader Esmail turned against the Aq-Qoyunlu and within a short space of time conquered huge swathes of territory, establishing an empire corresponding roughly to the territory of pre-Islamic Sassanid Iran. This achieved, Esmail declared immediately that Shi'ism would be the religion of his new empire.

Esmail did this in order to demand a higher level of commitment and allegiance to the new monarchy from his subjects and also to make a clear distinction between his empire and that of the Ottoman Turks, which was the prime state of Sunni Islam at the time, and Esmail's rival for supremacy in eastern Anatolia. Part of Esmail's intention was also to destabilize Ottoman rule there, in Anatolia, where there were many Shi'a Muslims. But Esmail and his followers were defeated at the battle of Chaldiran in 1514, where the wild Qezelbash cavalry were mown down in large numbers by Ottoman cannon. Thereafter Esmail's reputation for invincibility was somewhat dented. His ambitions and those of the dynasty for westward expansion into Anatolia faded, but the Safavids' commitment to Shi'ism (and a relatively extreme form of Shi'ism at that) endured. Having been a predominantly Sunni country before 1500, Iran became Shi'a, and has remained so.

What caused the collapse of the Safavid dynasty?

After the founder, Esmail, the greatest Shah of the Safavid dynasty was Shah Abbas, often called Shah Abbas the Great (Shah Abbas-e bozorg). He reigned from 1588 to 1629 and implemented wide-ranging reforms, creating a more centralized monarchical system, with many of the attributes of a modern state, including a core of troops for the army retained and paid as a standing force, and based in his new capital, Isfahan, plus a state bureaucracy for the collection and spending of tax revenue. He brought in large numbers of Christian Armenians and Georgians from the Caucasus to staff these new institutions, calculating that they would be more loyal to the monarchy than Qezelbash chiefs, for example. His policy deliberately weakened the Qezelbash, whose rivalries and infighting had been the main cause of the instability of the preceding period. His use of Christians in this way can also be interpreted as an emulation of Ottoman policy; since the previous century Ottoman successes and expansion had derived at least in part from a meritocratic system based on recruitment (abduction) of children from Christian communities in their Balkan provinces to serve as soldiers (the famous janissaries) and administrators. In Safavid service the Christians were supposed, at least for form's sake, to have converted to Islam; but many of the Georgians at least took names associated with the pre-Islamic legends of the *Shahnameh* like Rostam and Eskander, rather than Muslim names like Mohammad, Ali, or Hosein, and this may have signaled a certain ambiguity. It seems that they tended to revert to Christianity when they returned home.

Abbas also centralized more land under the power of the monarchy, taking it back from the Qezelbash, and reorganized the appointment of provincial governors so that governors served in each province for a limited time only. Previously Qezelbash, chiefs had treated governorships as personal property and had begun to expect to be able to pass them down in their own family; this had been, under earlier dynasties, one of the prime means by which central government had been destabilized, with old dynasties regularly being supplanted by new ones that had sprung up from provincial capitals. Abbas's policies to break the power of the Qezelbash and strengthen central authority were largely successful, and were made possible by the prestige he achieved in victorious war against the Ottomans. He took back Tabriz, and in the last years of his reign was able also to conquer Baghdad and most of what is now Iraq. Baghdad was lost again by his successor not long after Abbas's death, but Tabriz stayed under Persian rule.

The new pattern of government established by Abbas proved strong and durable. But the long-term effects of some of his policies were less benign (and it should be recognized that his efforts toward centralization, in such a large country with a relatively low average population density, harsh terrain, and diffuse and clustered economic activity, where so many other forces were centrifugal, were in any case an uphill struggle). All through his reign, and indeed through the period of Safavid rule as a whole, there was a tendency to reduce state support for the Sufis and to reinforce the monarchy's connections with, and support for, the Shi'a clergy. This policy paralleled the reduction in power of the Qezelbash, and other measures to broaden the monarchy's basis of support. To signal the policy and reinforce it, Shah Abbas himself made pilgrimages to shrine cities like Mashhad and gave money and property as endowments. Qom in particular, another shrine city, grew in importance as a center of clerical activity and theological study. The wealth and social position of the ulema were strengthened as other wealthy notables followed the Shah's example; the phenomenon continued long after Abbas's death and was encouraged further by the fact that property given to religious endowments was not subject to tax. A family with some clerics among its sons could thus give property to an endowment in effect as a tax-avoidance scheme; over decades the number of religious endowments proliferated. Unlike other property transfers, of course, gifts to religious endowments were permanent, so the overall effect for the monarchy, over time, was that a large part of the propertied wealth of the country was taken permanently out of tax, resulting in a significant loss of revenue to the state (something similar happened in Europe in the Middle Ages, in the centuries before the Protestant Reformation).

Another change that proved damaging in later decades was Abbas's move to keep heirs to the throne in the palace, within the harem. Before his time, royal princes had been given provincial governorships, often with a tutor to guide them, but this had contributed to civil strife as opposition factions had coalesced around the princes' provincial courts. In restricting princes to the palace, Abbas was again trying to protect the stability of the state; he was also, again, imitating contemporary Ottoman practice. But the result was a succession of weak Shahs, who came to the throne without the experience or the contacts to govern. There has sometimes been an Orientalizing tendency to see this development in terms of alcoholism and womanizing—while there is good evidence for both, the point is more that the princes tended to become, in some sense, institutionalized: self-indulgent, lazy, and malleable drones. In no monarchy would this have been a positive development.

The last decades of Safavid rule, at the end of the seventeenth century and the beginning of the eighteenth, were marked by weakness in the monarchy, damaging and divisive factionalism at court, and a phase of strong clerical power and influence, which was used to tighten clerical control over the conduct of women, and in some other ways prefigured the Islamic Republic of the late twentieth century. It was also a period of greater intolerance toward religious minorities, including Sufis, Hindus, Christians, Jews, and Sunni Muslims. This was particularly unfortunate and unwise, because the periphery of the empire was in many places dominated by militarily dangerous Sunni tribesmen who felt increasingly alienated by the sometimes aggressively intolerant attitudes encouraged by the Shi'a clergy. Prime among these warlike Sunni groups were the Afghans.

How did the Safavid dynasty fall and why was Nader Shah (reigned 1736–1747) significant?

The Safavid regime collapsed in 1722, after an Afghan revolt that began in Kandahar in 1709 culminated in a campaign westward by a smallish army of Afghan and Baluchi adventurers, who defeated a larger Safavid army at the battle of Golnabad and then besieged the capital, Isfahan. Isfahan capitulated in October 1722 and the last Safavid Shah abdicated in favor of the Afghan leader, Mahmud Ghilzai. But the Afghans had insufficient troops to take control of the whole Safavid Empire. Seeing their chance, the Ottomans occupied the western provinces, and the Russians moved into the territories on the southern shore of the Caspian Sea. In provinces like Khorasan and Fars local warlords took control. With this partition and widespread disarray it looked as though Iran might simply disappear, as Poland did for a time, later in the eighteenth century, partitioned between its neighbors.

The Afghans later murdered most of the Safavid royal family in Isfahan, but one prince, Tahmasp, had escaped during the siege. After adventures in which he fled from place to place in northern Persia with the Ottomans and Afghans in pursuit, he appeared in Khorasan with a few troops in 1726. There he was met by a local warlord, Nader Qoli, with more men, and between them they managed

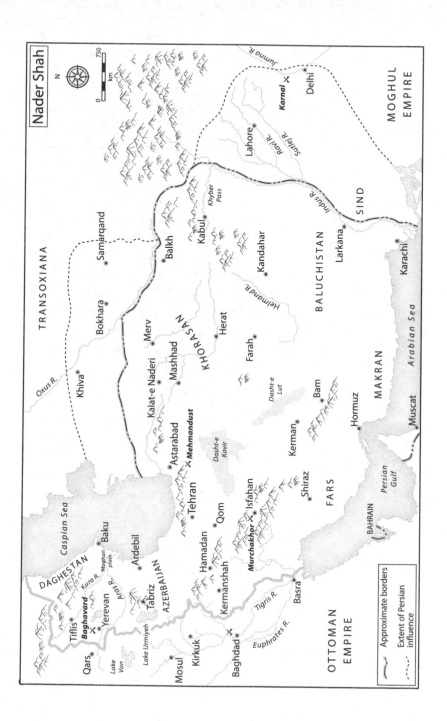

take the provincial capital, the shrine city of Mashhad. After a period of consolidation and recruitment, they moved against the Afghans, defeating them in three battles and retaking Isfahan from them at the end of 1729. Tahmasp was restored to the throne as Shah, but within a short time it became plain that Nader was the real power in the land. He deposed Tahmasp in 1732, and after a period as regent, made himself Shah in his own right in 1736. This usurpation was made possible by his victories over the Afghans and Ottomans, through which he restored the frontiers of Persia to their positions before 1722. After becoming Shah, he moved east, reconquering Kandahar before marching his troops into Moghul territory in early 1739, defeating the Moghul Shah and occupying Delhi. This victory brought Nader's rise to wider attention, including in Europe. He perpetrated a massacre of perhaps thirty thousand people in Delhi (after rioting broke out and some of his men were killed by the crowds) and extorted an enormous treasure which, with some difficulty, he transported back to his base in Khorasan.

Nader's military successes were in part the result of brilliant generalship, but were also achieved by careful preparation, logistical planning, and innovation. His armies developed further the changes made by Abbas the Great, to make firearms standard for all troops for the first time, and to make firepower the main battle-winning weapon. His troops were retained on a standing basis, trained and drilled to use the muskets, and he also (particularly in the 1740s) established a powerful artillery corps. The army grew from 20,000 in the late 1720s to a maximum of perhaps 375,000 in the early 1740s. These developments were hugely expensive, and there is evidence that he began administrative and fiscal reforms to support them. These phenomena—and other features of Nader's reign—are strongly reminiscent of what in the historiography of the early modern era in Europe has been called the Military Revolution (albeit limited, obviously, by the short duration of his reign): a complex of developments which, according to the theory, in Europe eventually brought about the modern nation-state. Nader's relentless tribal policy, aimed at weakening the independence of the tribes, bending them to his will and exercising central control over them, was a parallel development and a significant harbinger of developments later, in the reign of Reza Shah in the twentieth century (though Reza Shah's methods were different).

Up to the late 1730s, many Iranians welcomed Nader's rise to power because he restored order following the chaos of the Afghan revolt and the collapse of Safavid authority. He was regarded as a harsh ruler but a fair and ruthlessly effective one, at a time when the country was confronted by formidable enemies and demanded firm rule. In many of his policies, notably his religious policy, he made a deliberate effort to signal a break with the abuses and the failures of the last Safavids; his policies can indeed be read in part as a critique of the late-Safavid style of government. But he always had a brutal streak and from the time of his return from India onward, although his prestige and power had never been greater, the quality of his rule deteriorated. It seems he was ill with some form of liver disease, but the crucial event was his blinding of his son Reza Qoli Mirza in the autumn of 1742 (Nader believed his son had plotted to kill him). After that, remorse and recurring rages, probably fueled by excessive drinking that further exacerbated his liver complaint, led him in a downward spiral that could only have one outcome. He imposed enormous tax demands on his subjects, including some of his closest adherents, and punished them with extreme cruelty if they protested or otherwise failed to pay. Economic conditions and the living conditions of most people deteriorated.

There were a series of revolts in the mid-1740s that Nader crushed with extreme violence, and in June 1747 he was murdered by his own bodyguard.

This analysis, which makes the link to the Military Revolution in Europe, is not accepted by all historians of Iran—some of whom find the facts of Nader's reign rebarbative. The history of the wars of the sixteenth, seventeenth, and eighteenth centuries in Europe is, of course, scarcely less brutal and unpleasant, if we look at the detail below the familiar baroque surface. Nader Shah's reign has been rather neglected by historians, but to do so risks distorting the possibilities and therefore the reality of the period, and what came later. It was not inevitable that Iran had to become the victim of domineering European powers in the nineteenth century. Other outcomes were possible.

After Nader's death, there was civil war, economic disruption, impoverishment, misery, and emigration. It has been estimated that Iran's population declined from around nine million at the beginning of the century to six million at the end. A degree of stability was restored in the 1760s and 1770s by Karim Khan Zand, who ruled the southern and western provinces of the country from Shiraz (without ever taking the title of Shah). He had been one of Nader's officers; other former lieutenants set up new kingdoms in Georgia and Afghanistan. But in the 1780s there was civil war again as Karim Khan's successors in the south struggled for supremacy with the Qajar tribe from the north. Eventually, the Qajar leader, Agha Mohammad Khan, won the struggle and had himself made Shah in 1796. It seems he modeled himself to some extent on Nader Shah; unfortunately he took after him in brutality as well as in his military talents, and like Nader he was murdered by some of his own people in 1797. But he had succeeded in establishing his family in the monarchy; his nephew Fath Ali Shah took the throne and ruled until 1834.

Did contact with Europe benefit or damage Iran in the nineteenth century?

Before the 1790s there was little contact between Iran and the countries of Europe. Even with Russia, the state geographically nearest, contact had been spasmodic. There had been Dutch and English trading missions on the Persian Gulf coast, the Portuguese had dominated the Hormuz strait by means of their fort on Hormuz Island in the sixteenth and early seventeenth centuries, and there were European visitors, merchants, and missionaries; but much of this activity ceased with the trauma and economic disruption of the eighteenth century, especially after 1747.

In 1783 Erekle II, the king of Georgia, agreed a treaty with Russia, making Georgia a Russian protectorate. Erekle had earlier been one of Nader Shah's officers, and had accompanied him on his campaign to Delhi. Presumably, given the persistent instability in Persia, Erekle had decided that protection from his Russian co-religionists was a safer bet. Unfortunately for the Georgians, Agha Mohammad Khan marched his troops into Georgia and destroyed the city of Tiflis in 1795, taking away fifteen thousand women and children as captives. The Russians responded by occupying Georgia in 1799, later annexing the territory altogether. Ambitious Russian commanders looked on the Caucasus as a theater for further Russian expansion; Fath Ali Shah continued to regard Georgia as an Iranian province. War was the outcome. The two wars that followed, in 1804–1813 and 1826–1828, proved conclusively that Iran could not match Russia as a military power. Despite some successes in both wars, the Iranian armies (despite efforts to catch up) were outclassed in efficiency, drill, training, and staff work. In addition, Russian reserves in manpower and logistics were enough to overwhelm the Iranian forces. It was not just the army: Russia was simply bigger and had developed (in competition with her European rivals) into a

Qajar & Modern Iran
Showing traditional tribal & linguistic regions

pre-1801 border
1813 border
1828 border

Note:
The borders of Persia in the northeast
and east were defined by agreements
with Russia and Britain in the latter
part of the nineteenth century.

RUSSIA

RUSSIA

GEORGIA

DAGHESTAN

Tiflis

Darband

Yerevan

Baku

Lake
Van

Qajar

Aslanduz

Talish

Aras R.

Caspian
Sea

Turkmen

Merv

Qajar

Ardebil

Tabriz

Urmiyeh

Azeri

Gilaki

Resht

Ashkhabad

Afshar

Jalayir

Maragha

Afshar

Zanjan

Mazandarani

Qajar

Yomut

Astarabad

Quchan

Kurds

Nishapur

Afshar

Mashhad

Qazvin

KURDISTAN

Kurdish

Tehran

Afshar

KHORASAN

Hamadan

Qom

Dasht-e Kavir

Herat

Qasr-e-Shirin

Kermanshah

Saltanabad

Kashan

Tabas

Abdali

Baghdad

Lur

Borujerd

Arab

Birjand

AFGHANISTAN

LORESTAN

Bakhtiari

Isfahan

Dasht-e Lut

SISTAN

Tigris R.

Dezful

Masjed-e-Soleiman

Yazd

Shushtar

Ahwaz

Kerman

PAKISTAN

Euphrates R.

Basra

Arab

Qashqai

Afshar

Bam

OTTOMAN EMPIRE

Mohammerah
(Khorramshahr)

Shiraz

Baluch

N

Bushire

FARS

Bampur

Bandar Abbas

MAKRAN

Lingeh

Arab

Persian
Gulf

Jask

Chahbahar

0   175

km

Gulf of Oman

new kind of state, more centralized and better organized for war—the sort of state that could, ultimately, have developed in Iran from Nader Shah's innovations, but had not.

The treaties of Golestan and Turkmanchai, in 1813 and 1828, respectively, were a major national humiliation. In addition to Georgia, Iran lost the territories of what are today Armenia, Daghestan, Nagorno-Karabagh, and the independent state of Azerbaijan, with its capital in Baku. Some of these territories (notably Daghestan) had been troublesome, but in general, compared with much of the rest of Iran, they were rich, well-populated, developed regions with relatively high rainfall and productive agriculture.

But that was not the full extent of the humiliation. The Iranians were compelled by the Turkmanchai treaty to render back Christian captives taken since 1795, to pay a large cash sum as a war indemnity, to accept trading treaties favorable to Russia, to grant Russian citizens in Iran immunity from local legal proceedings (these were called capitulation rights), and to give Russian consular officials free access all over the country. There was even a clause that implied Russian oversight over accession of future monarchs to the throne of Persia.

The latter clauses in particular set the scene for the further humiliations and losses of sovereignty over the next hundred years. Other European powers, notably the British, sought and obtained the preferential arrangements the Russians had obtained for their merchants and other citizens.

Part of the story of the failure of Qajar Iran in the wars with Russia at the beginning of the nineteenth century had been the role played by the other European powers, France and Britain, who at this time were locked in mutual enmity in what have since been called the Napoleonic Wars. At different times, both had signed treaties of alliance with the Qajar monarchy, only to renege on them or evade their commitments when Fath Ali Shah asked for help against the Russians. In particular, Napoleon had agreed to help Iran under the Treaty of Finkenstein in May 1807, only to turn his back on the Iranians a few months later, in July, when he signed the Treaty of Tilsit with Russia. Britain then made a treaty of alliance with Persia (in 1809) but went much cooler about military help after 1812, when Napoleon went to war with Russia again, and Britain became an ally of the Tsar. Later, at the time of the Treaty of Turkmanchai, Britain offered help as a mediator, but acted more in the Russian interest than for the Persians.

The underlying fact was that whereas Fath Ali Shah was looking for a reliable ally to help him against the Russians, Russia was a much more valuable potential ally for France or Britain than Persia. Qajar Iran had tried to engage with the Europeans as an equal, but had lacked the necessary military clout, and had not been treated like one. Fath Ali Shah had only slowly learned the rules of the diplomatic game, discovering belatedly how heavily weighted against him they were. This humiliating subordinate position was emphasized again and again later in the century in Iran's dealings with Britain and Russia.

In 1838 and again in 1856 Fath Ali Shah's successors tried to retake Herat, which had belonged to Iran before 1747, but the British intervened to prevent that. All through the nineteenth century the British wanted to protect the borders of India, and were fearful that the Russians might use Persian territory to encroach. Iran was caught between the two powers, powerless herself to stop them meddling, but in need of their help to facilitate economic development. The Shah also needed them for loans, because his expenditure exceeded his income, and (principally because he continued to lack the troops necessary to impose his will outside Tehran) his ability to extract taxation from his subjects was minimal.

In 1872 the Baron de Reuter (the founder of Reuters news agency among many other business interests), with luke-warm support from the British government, made an agree-ment with Naser od-Din Shah to begin a sweeping range of developmental projects in Iran, on a monopoly basis, including mining, factories, and, above all, a railway from the Caspian to the coast of the Persian Gulf. In return, de Reuter gave the Shah £40,000. But the Russians opposed the deal and there was opposition within the country. The Shah eventually cancelled the concession, but kept the money; a dispute rumbled on for years until (in 1889) de Reuter abandoned his claims in return for the right to set up the Imperial Bank of Persia, with monopoly rights to print the national currency. In the interim, the Russians brought for-ward rival suggestions for railway construction, but were stymied by British intervention. Elsewhere in the world at this time, especially in new territories in the Americas and in Asian Russia, railway infrastructure brought huge economic and developmental benefits, opening up the new territories and driving rapid development. But in Iran, where the great distances, difficult terrain, and the isolation of urban centers had been a barrier to economic develop-ment and integration for centuries, and railways could have brought huge benefits, no railways were built.

By this time, underlying conditions in the Iranian econ-omy had changed in response to an increasing penetra-tion of markets by foreign goods. Many Iranian products proved unable to compete with cheap imports (especially food staples like grain and sugar; and textiles), so agricul-ture reoriented to produce cash crops for export (cotton and opium for example). The reduced capacity for domestic food production contributed to a number of severe fam-ines, especially in 1870–1871, in which it has been estimated that up to a tenth of the population perished. Famines were repeated again later, notably during the First World War. The economic changes left many people angry (especially bazaaris) and contributed to the opposition to the Reuter concession.

In 1879 the Shah was able to achieve a partial remedy for his lack of military force by setting up, with Russian help, a unit called the Cossack Brigade. For the remaining period of Qajar rule, the Cossack Brigade was the most important single military force under the Shah's authority. Eventually it grew to (at least nominally) division strength, but even so it never numbered more than six thousand to eight thousand troops at most: utterly inadequate to control a territory the size of Iran. The ordinary soldiers in the brigade were Iranians, but the officers were Russians; and this meant that the unit's loyalty to the Shah was doubtful at best, should the Shah want to act against the interests of the Russian Tsar. As the reign of Naser od-Din Shah drew on he grew increasingly conservative, increasingly disillusioned with the British, and increasingly aligned with the Russian interest in Iran in any case.

In the early 1890s a dispute over a tobacco monopoly repeated some of the features of the Reuters Concession episode. In 1890 the Shah granted monopoly rights to a British entrepreneur, Major Talbot, that enabled him to buy, sell, and export tobacco in Iran without competition. This drew opposition from a formidable alliance of opponents: from landlords and tobacco growers, who found themselves forced to sell at a fixed price; from bazaar traders, who saw themselves frozen out of another lucrative sector of the economy; from the readership of new reform and nationalist-oriented newspapers operating from overseas; and from the ulema, who were closely aligned to the bazaar traders and disliked the foreign presence in the country on principle. This alliance of interests became the classic pattern, repeated in later movements.

Mass protests against the concession took place in most of the major cities in 1891, culminating in something like a revolt in Tabriz and a demonstration in Tehran that was fired on by troops, leading to further demonstrations. The clerics organized a boycott, which was so successful that the Shah was forced early in 1892 to cancel the concession, incurring a large debt.

Foreign interference, loss of territory, loss of sovereignty, loss of economic autonomy, loss of prestige and authority on the part of the monarchy and government: indignation at these developments and a growing nationalist solidarity against them among key social groups (notably clergy, bazaaris, and a new, growing class of western-influenced intellectuals): these were the features and the consequences of Iran's contact with Europe in the nineteenth century.

How did the Shi'a clergy become so potentially powerful in nineteenth-century Iran?

Until 1924, when Kemal Atatürk abolished it, the caliphate was the ultimate religious authority in Sunni Muslim countries (some have suggested that the emergence of theologically illiterate groups like Al-Qaeda and the Islamic State in recent years has been facilitated by the vacuum this abolition created). But Iran, after the establishment of Shi'ism as the dominant faith by the Safavids in the sixteenth century, followed a separate path. Until the collapse of Safavid authority in 1722, the Shi'a clergy were close to the monarchy, but they were implicated in the Safavids' fall and their interests were damaged by the chaos that followed—and perhaps above all by Nader Shah's confiscation of religious property. In the following decades many clerics emigrated to India, to Ottoman Iraq, or to the southern shore of the Persian Gulf.

Yet from this low point the power and influence of the Shi'a clergy grew until in 1979 a cleric, claiming to speak for all, took over supreme authority in the country. How did this happen? It began with a dispute within the body of the ulema about the essentials of the role of the clergy themselves, which came to a head toward the end of the eighteenth century (though the origins of the dispute went back much earlier). There were two factions—the *Akhbari* and the *Usuli*. The Akhbari said that each Muslim had in the Qoran and the other traditional texts (the *hadith*) all he needed for his guidance, and that there was only a limited place, if any, for the interpretation of religious law based on reason (*ijtihad*)—a position that was close to the traditional line of Sunni Islam on these matters. The Usuli argued the contrary: that ijtihad was legitimate and necessary to reinterpret religious law afresh in each generation, in the light of new circumstances and new understanding, and that only trained, learned ulema (*mojtahed*) could be trusted to do this.

By the early nineteenth century the Usulis had won the argument (under the leadership of the great *mojtahed* Agha Mohammad Baqer Behbehani, who lived from around 1706 to 1790). Akhbarism was pushed to the margins, and a new arrangement developed, according to which ordinary Muslims gave their allegiance—and often, a portion of their material earnings—to the ulema. In each generation, among the whole body of mojtahed, one or two clerics emerged to serve as a supreme guide to other ulema and to ordinary Muslims in religious matters. Such a cleric was called a *marja-e taqlid* (source of emulation), or *marja*. The marja passed down judgments to lesser clerics in response to questions or requests for advice passed up to him, and more junior clerics across the country forwarded money upward too. The senior clerics naturally acquired prestige and influence with each request they answered, and with each parcel of cash. This meant that, without any explicit plan or blueprint, the Shi'a clergy developed a religious hierarchy, analogous to that of other religions—to that of the Catholic church, for example—but quite unlike the looser arrangements of Sunni Islam. As time went on and more ambitious young men strove to qualify as mojtahed, new, more elevated levels of dignity were added to distinguish between the clerics—*hojjatoleslam* (proof of Islam) and *ayatollah* (sign of God). This system helped the ulema to reassert their social authority and to restore their wealth, as a class: this time quite independently of secular rulers, at a time (the nineteenth century) when the monarchy was relatively weak.

Shari'a—religious law—is meant to govern every aspect of a Muslim's life. Religious law has a wider significance in Islam than in Christianity and most other religions, giving clerics a role much more important than that of mere prayer-leaders in the mosque. They were arbitrators in family or business or other legal disputes and also acted as judges in criminal cases. They served as notaries for official documents. Often they were the only authority figures in smaller towns or villages, and acted effectively as governors, perhaps in association with elders or village headmen. In the larger towns and cities the ulema had close connections with the merchants and craftsmen of the bazaars, who gained and kept status there not just through their wealth but also through a reputation for piety and religious respectability, and often demonstrated that piety by giving money for religious purposes—for example to repair the roof of a mosque or to help pay for a religious school (*madreseh*). Bazaari and ulema families often intermarried. Between them, the ulema and the bazaaris formed the dominant urban class and came to be of central importance in politics from the end of the nineteenth century onward. Through the religious hierarchy, the contacts established during their long training, and family connections, the ulema had access to a network of clergy and ordinary Muslims across the whole country and beyond.

The clergy's position in Iranian society meant that when secular authority failed or was challenged, ordinary people naturally turned to the ulema for guidance. Senior clerics repeatedly emerged as leaders of political dissent. This happened in 1890–1892, in 1905–1906, in 1951–1953 (to a more limited extent), in 1963, and of course in 1978–1979. They were able to communicate and coordinate action with other ulema, and to spread propaganda, often using new technology (in 1892, the telegraph system; in 1978, cassette tapes and photocopiers). Their religious authority gave them advantages by comparison with other potential leaders of mass movements; it gave them a degree of immunity from repression. Secular rulers found it difficult, and often counterproductive, to act even against individual mullahs. Sometimes such action was impossible anyway—the most senior marjas were often out of reach of the Iranian government altogether, living in Najaf or one of the other shrine cities of Iraq.

What were the origins and what was the significance of the Constitutional Revolution 1906–1911?

The first great revolution of the twentieth century in Iran, which began in the years 1905–1906, had both long-term and short-term causes. The long-term causes included several phenomena we have discussed already: disillusionment with the Qajar monarchy, and resentment at foreign interference in Iran. But the class interests of the clergy and the bazaaris, the most articulate and wealthy social groups in the country, were also important. Both felt that western encroachment had eroded their traditional positions and privileges.

By the beginning of the twentieth century a high proportion of Iran's foreign trade, including the import of many staple foods, came through Russia. The abortive Russian revolution of 1905 disrupted this trade and caused rapid price rises; wheat prices went up by 90 percent and sugar prices by 33 percent in the cities of northern Iran in the early part of 1905. As well as causing distress to ordinary people, the slump in trade hit the Qajar government too, because its finances were heavily dependent on receipts from customs duties (administered by a Belgian, Monsieur Naus). There were demonstrations in the summer of 1905 and again in December: in the latter case after two sugar merchants were beaten at the orders of the governor of Tehran for alleged profiteering. The demonstrators, led by two distinguished clerics, demanded the removal of the governor and of foreigners from positions of influence, the enforcement of shari'a law, and the establishment of a House of Justice (*adalatkhaneh*). What this last should be was not clear at first—the clerics probably had in mind a relatively small advisory body of notables representing the views and wishes of the clerical and middle classes. The Shah eventually had to give in, but over the following months reforms were not brought forward, and demonstrations were renewed in the summer of 1906. This time senior clerics withdrew to Qom, while bazaaris, religious students, and others took refuge in the grounds of the British legation in Golhak, then to the north of Tehran, with the consent of the British diplomats there. This time they would not be fobbed off with mere promises, and they did not disperse.

The initial grievances and requirements of the demonstrators reflected the attitudes and interests of the clerical and bazaari classes they came from, and were essentially conservative, paradoxical though that may seem for what became a revolutionary movement. They wanted a stronger government that would take their wishes into account, that would resist foreign influence and reestablish what they saw as the traditional order; the bazaaris wanted an end to monopolies, concessions, and other privileges for foreigners that excluded them from lucrative sectors of the economy, and the clergy wanted to roll back western cultural and intellectual influence (they disliked the Shah's trips to Europe and his hobnobbing with European royalty, and also the presence in Iran of schools opened with the Shah's permission and run by European and American Christian missionaries).

But as the demonstrations continued over the summer of 1906, other voices began to be heard, especially in the gatherings at the British legation, where the numbers eventually grew to around fourteen thousand. Over the previous half century, a small new class of educated, western-influenced professionals had sprung up: some from clerical or bazaari families, others from junior branches of the Qajar nobility (the young Mohammad Mosaddeq, for example). In the time of Naser od-Din Shah, their ideas had been stimulated and sustained by clandestine journals (*Qanun, Akhtar*) published outside Iran in Persian and smuggled in. After Naser od-Din Shah was assassinated in 1896 his son Mozaffar od-Din Shah relaxed previous censorship restrictions, permitting the establishment of newspapers and some political societies (*anjoman*). The revolution released a new wave of journalistic and political activity; the number of newspapers jumped from six to over a hundred. Much of this activity showed the influence of western ideas—particularly for political liberty, representative government, and the rule of law. The province of Azerbaijan and the city of Tabriz were particularly important in these developments because they were physically closer to Turkey and Russia and more open to outside influence—including even socialist ideas developed from contact with social democrats in Russian Azerbaijan.

Over the summer of 1906 these kinds of speakers exerted influence over the crowds at Golhak, and some of the more influential clerics, at least, were sympathetic to their ideas. The call for a House of Justice developed into a demand for an elected Parliament and a full-blown European-style constitution, signifying for the first time the establishment of the rule of law and a limited, constitutional monarchy.

Mozaffar od-Din Shah prevaricated, but time was not on his side. His financial position worsened further as, with the bazaars closed, the economy ground to a halt and his customs revenues dried up. He was also very ill. The constitutionalists were obdurate and eventually he agreed to allow an assembly to convene to draft a constitution. This took place from October 1906; the constitution was presented to the Shah when it was ready and he finally signed it on December 30. Five days later the Shah was dead (the last Iranian monarch to die in Iran, as Shah), but Iran had a constitution and a Parliament (Majles).

Although subsequent developments were complex and the constitution was often flouted or abused, it remained an important feature of Iranian politics and remained in place until the revolution of 1979. After 1906 there was a split in the revolutionary movement as some clergy reacted against the western-inspired reform program of the new constitutionalist government, and turned back toward the reactionary monarchist side. Mozaffar od-Din Shah's successor, Mohammad Ali Shah, was determined to restore untrammeled autocratic rule and had the support of the Russians too. He carried out a coup in 1908. The constitutionalists in the provinces marched on Tehran the following year and reestablished their government, sending Mohammad into exile, but there was more infighting and violence, and the constitutionalist experiment was finally brought to an end by a further coup in 1911, which put Mohammad Ali's young son Ahmad Shah on the throne.

It is sometimes said, in ignorance, that there is no democratic tradition in Iran or in the Middle East. But in the case of Iran at least, that is untrue. Despite the apparent failure of the revolution, the constitutionalist movement changed everything in Iranian politics. There could be no going back. It set up a solid body of nationalist, liberal principles for political and press freedoms, for representative government, and for resistance to foreign encroachment that largely set the agenda for Iranian politics over the next hundred years.

3

THE PAHLAVIS

How did the British take control of Iranian oil in
the first years of the twentieth century?

Part of the story of western encroachment and the increasing weakness of the Qajar monarchy in the latter part of the nineteenth century was the long list of concessions—monopoly deals granted to foreigners allowing them to operate in the Iranian economy under privileged conditions, in return for a lump sum payment or a loan, or some other mixed arrangement. Europeans regarded this kind of exploitative deal as normal—they were engaged in Egypt and elsewhere in the Middle East on a similar basis.

The Reuters Concession of the 1870s and the tobacco monopoly of the early 1890s failed, but others were more successful, and in 1901 a British entrepreneur who had made his first fortune in Australia, William Knox D'Arcy, agreed to pay £20,000 in cash and £20,000 in stocks in return for rights to explore in search of oil in southern Iran. The concession further provided that if oil were discovered, the Persian government would get 16 percent of the profits.

After the deal was signed D'Arcy waited impatiently year after year as test drillings repeatedly failed and costs rose. In 1904–1905, with bankruptcy threatening, he had to take an extra £100,000 from the Burmah Oil Company (through the mediation of British naval officials) to enable him to continue. By 1908 the money was running out again, the revolution that had erupted in Persia in 1905–1906 was making the project look increasingly uncertain, and Burmah were threatening to pull out. So when the news reached London that the last test drilling near Masjed-e Soleiman in Khuzestan had finally produced a gusher of oil on May 26 1908, D'Arcy and the directors of Burmah Oil were both delighted and much relieved. Within a few months they established the Anglo-Persian Oil Company (APOC) to exploit the find (D'Arcy remained a director until he died in 1917).

The involvement of the British Navy in the talks between D'Arcy and Burmah was significant. In 1908 the Royal Navy still ran on coal, but had already decided on a switch to oil, which burned more efficiently. By the outbreak of the First World War, most British battleships were oil-fueled—but at that time Britain possessed no known oil reserves of her own. The Iranian oilfields offered the most plentiful supply for the Royal Navy. Drawing on the well at Masjed-e Soleiman, a new refinery at Abadan was producing 2,400 barrels of oil per day by 1912 and 20,000 per day by 1918. To secure this supply Winston Churchill in 1914 masterminded the purchase of a controlling share in APOC for the British government.

For years the British government had been involved in Persia and Central Asia to prevent other European powers, especially the Russians, from threatening British India, but by 1908 the strategic emphasis had shifted. Having been uneasy rivals in Asia for much of the nineteenth century, the British and Russians found themselves allies, with France, at the beginning of the twentieth; they were brought together by the increasing threat from Germany. For the British this was (again) mainly about ships; the Germans were deliberately building a fleet to challenge the global dominance of the Royal Navy. Faced with this new situation the British and Russians settled their old quarrels, and in 1907 made a treaty establishing spheres of influence within Iran. The Iranians were not consulted. The Russians got the north, and the British the southeast, adjacent to the border of British India. The British sector was quickly extended westward after 1908 to include the newly discovered oilfields. From this point on Britain's prime interest in Iran was oil.

Although the Russians succeeded in ousting the constitutionalists and in reinstating a monarchist government in the name of Ahmad Shah in Tehran in December 1911, most of the country remained beyond its control: lawless or dominated by tribal chiefs. The outbreak of the First World War deepened the chaos, as Turks, Russians, Germans, British, local revolutionaries, monarchists, tribes, and (later) Bolshevik forces fought each other sporadically over Iranian territory—another testament to the impotence of the Qajar government, which had declared an optimistic neutrality in 1914.

Did the British put Reza Khan in power in 1921?
Was he a British stooge?

In the early stages of the First World War in Iran, the British lost ground (in 1915–1916), but kept their grip on Khuzestan and the oilfields. By the war's end the British had come out on top, because most of their opponents had been defeated, but they were not in control. They had four small armed groups in the country, but the great distances, poor roads, and continuing instability meant those forces were almost unable to communicate with each other. The country was in a desperate state; law and order had broken down, trade had slumped; disease and famine had caused widespread loss of life. In London Lord Curzon, the Foreign Secretary, insisted that Iran should come under British political control, according to the terms of an Anglo-Persian agreement, which was signed in 1919 between the British and Ahmad Shah's ministers. But the agreement never entered into force, because the Majles, true to the principles the constitutionalists had asserted in 1906, refused to ratify it. British commanders on the ground in Iran began to realize that whatever Lord Curzon might think, a more limited solution had to be found, more focused on the essential British interest—oil—and more manageable given the very limited military force available to the British in Iran.

As the impasse over the Anglo-Persian agreement persisted toward the end of 1920, overall command of British troops in Iran passed to General Edmund Ironside, a man with a decisive and independent frame of mind. Without consulting London, Ironside found a solution to the British predicament that would enable him to withdraw British troops safely from most of the country. The Cossacks, expanded to weak division strength during the war, still had Russian officers (marooned in Iran after the revolution of 1917). Ironside removed them and appointed Iranians from the ranks in their place. He then selected one of them, Reza Khan, as the de facto commander, and gave him to understand that if he were to march on Tehran and set up a military government, British forces would not stand in his way.

In February 1921 Reza Khan did just that, and set up a new government in association with a mixed group of nationalists and former constitutionalists. British troops withdrew (except in the southwest, around the oil fields). Less than five years later, having defeated various separatists, rebels, and tribal warlords in the provinces (and after attempting to set up a republic), Reza Khan had himself crowned as the first Shah of a new dynasty, the Pahlavi dynasty.

So Reza Shah came to power with tacit support from the local British commander, but against the policy of the British imperial government in London. His accession was in fact the product of contingent and passing local conditions, and once in power he did not govern under British direction or, necessarily, in accordance with British interests. He was preoccupied with establishing Iran as an independent, modern country, leaving behind the weakness and humiliation of the Qajar period, and the chaos and lawlessness of the decade after 1911. He was more influenced by the example of Turkey under Atatürk, and perhaps of the Tsarist Russian officers he served under in the Cossack division, than by the British. He had many differences with the constitutionalists; his instincts were authoritarian and illiberal. But he shared with them a strong Iranian nationalism and a deep-seated suspicion of British motives.

Were Reza Shah's efforts to develop and modernize Iran a success or a failure?

Once established in power, Reza Shah's first and overriding priority was to establish a strong, effective, modern army. The army was to be the prime means of developing the country on a western model, and also the prime beneficiary of that development. With effective armed forces he could control the territory of Iran properly, and collect taxation comprehensively—something the Qajars had never done successfully. With a properly functioning tax structure, he could regularize the finances of the state, and (with the help of the oil revenue) invest: in the army itself, but also in justice, health, education, and roads and railways. He attempted to make the economy more independent by encouraging investment in import-substitution industries. By the end of the 1930s he had built nearly 20,000 kilometers of roads, and 1,500 kilometers of railways; total school attendance had gone from 55,000 to over 457,000. The army had expanded from under 10,000 men to around 100,000, with a larger number of reservists, and was equipped with modern artillery, some tanks, and aircraft.

Through the 1920s and 1930s Reza Shah used the army to establish his authority throughout the country, forcing tribal groups to submit, abandon their nomadic way of life, and settle in villages. The policy was unpopular with the tribes (especially when combined with conscription) but not with the rest of the populace, who disliked the tribes' traditional disposition to lawlessness and brigandage, and blamed the interference of some of their leaders in politics for some of the traumas of the period after the Constitutional Revolution.

But other aspects of Reza Shah's rule were less successful, and by the end of his reign he was unpopular with most sections of Iranian society. Perhaps the most obvious failure was his unsuccessful effort to renegotiate the terms of the oil concession under which APOC (which became AIOC—the Anglo-Iranian Oil Company—after 1935) operated. After a period of tension (and unilateral abrogation of the concession) in the early 1930s, Reza Shah had to accept a meager improvement that still yielded him only 20 percent of profits (in place of the previous 16 percent). This was a continuing humiliation, as well as a damaging economic and financial loss. Reza Shah's model, Atatürk, did not have to tolerate any such alien interference in his country. Reza Shah's reform of education and law, and his enforcement of a western-style dress code, were in line with an Atatürk-style secularizing, modernizing policy, but alienated the ulema, who remained much more influential than their counterparts in Turkey. Their aversion to western-inspired innovations was shared by many ordinary Iranians, in particular the bazaaris, who also disliked his introduction of state monopolies in some sectors of the economy. Liberal constitutionalists resented his abuse of the constitution, his denial of political freedom of expression, his manipulation of elections, and his execution of several eminent former politicians, including his court minister, Teymourtash (although an authoritarian, Atatürk in Turkey maintained a functioning democratic element in the system he controlled). Improvements in health and education were real, but confined largely to the main cities, while the majority of the population remained rural, poor, and subject to unhealthy and primitive conditions. Reza Shah railroaded his often reluctant countrymen into change, and brought them many benefits, many of which were only fully appreciated in the longer term. But his achievement fell short even by his own standard, and even more so in the political sphere.

Why did the British and Russians occupy Iran and depose Reza Shah in 1941?

Reza Shah made use of foreign technical assistance in many of his infrastructure and other development projects, but he was wary of the colonial powers that had meddled in such a damaging way in Iran in the Qajar period, and avoided asking for help from the British or the Russians. Many Iranians shared his attitudes; young men who studied at universities abroad often preferred to go to France. In the mid-1920s he employed an American financial adviser, Arthur Millspaugh (who eventually left after arguing with the Shah over the amounts of money he wanted to spend on the army). German engineers helped the Shah build roads and bridges, and German scholars advised him on language reform to remove words of non-Persian origin. These scholars, in the 1930s, were keen on racial theories of Aryanism; as discussed earlier, Persian has a common Indo-European root with Latin, Greek,

Sanskrit, English, and German. Building on all this, some have portrayed Reza Shah as a kind of Fascist dictator like Franco, Mussolini, or Hitler, but despite some of the similarities that one can attribute to the spirit of the times, that is overdrawn.

When the British and Russians invaded and occupied Iran in August 1941, the immediate pretext was that, despite Iran's declared neutrality, Reza Shah was too pro-German and had refused to expel German technicians and advisers. But there were relatively few of these in the country and it has been suggested that the British were more concerned that there could be a pro-German coup *against* the Shah, similar to the one that had recently removed the pro-British king in Iraq. Before Hitler's invasion of the Soviet Union in June 1941, with the Nazi-Soviet non-aggression pact in place and the United States still neutral, Britain's position in the Middle East was shaky, especially after the successes of Rommel, the Italians, and the Afrika Korps in North Africa in March–April 1941, and the coup in Iraq (April 1). After Hitler invaded Russia, Churchill moved quickly to negotiate strategic projects of cooperation with the Soviets. Reflecting Britain's continuing preoccupation with the Iranian oilfields, at the top of the list was joint occupation of Iran. For the Russians, the important benefit was the opening up of a new route by which to receive vital war materials. These were desperately needed as Hitler conquered more and more Soviet territory and captured more and more Red Army units with their equipment over the summer.

In that context, it is plain that the invasion and occupation of Iran in 1941 was dictated more by the cold strategic necessities of the new Allies than by an assessment of Reza Shah's pro-German sympathies. The army on which Reza Shah had lavished so much attention was capable of no more than a token resistance, and the British and Russian forces met in Tehran in September. Reza Shah abdicated on condition that his son Mohammad Reza would take his place as Shah, and went into exile in South Africa, where he died in 1944.

How and why was Prime Minister Mosaddeq removed from power in 1953?

By accident rather than design, Iran's occupation by the Allies during the Second World War fostered an intense mood of nationalism. The country was occupied by foreign troops, but within the parameters of occupation, press freedom was permitted once more—more free than in the time of Reza Shah. There was a new outpouring of journalistic and political activity, as before the revolution of 1906. As elsewhere at the time, and especially in France (a spiritual second home for many educated Iranians of this generation) much of this activity was left-leaning and pro-communist; and this was also the period of greatest growth, and greatest influence, of the leftist Tudeh party. Tudeh began as a home-grown Social Democratic party (in 1941) but quickly came under Soviet control.

In 1945 the political focus was on the delay in the withdrawal of Soviet forces from Azerbaijan and Kurdestan, in the northwest of the country. After Soviet forces finally withdrew at the end of 1946, the nationalists' attention turned to their other great grievance; British control of the Iranian oil industry.

Mohammad Mosaddeq belonged to an older generation of Iranian politicians. From an aristocratic family descended (like many others) from Fath Ali Shah, he had been educated in Paris and Switzerland and was a member of the first Majles under the constitution of 1906. Having been out of sympathy with Reza Shah, he returned to Iran after Reza Shah's abdication in 1941 and was elected to the

Majles again in 1944, becoming leader of the National Front coalition (Jebhe Melli).

Mosaddeq was appointed prime minister at the end of April 1951 (after his predecessor, Ali Razmara, had been assassinated) and on May 1 the Shah approved legislation framed by Mosaddeq to nationalize the oil industry (a bill approving nationalization in principle had been passed by the Majles on March 15). Nationalization of oil was wildly popular in Iran, but profoundly unwelcome to the British government—in the years after the Second World War cheap oil was more vital than ever to the floundering British economy. In Britain, Mosaddeq was depicted as an erratic and untrustworthy demagogue. Negotiations between the Iranians and the British for amicable settlement of the dispute were renewed after nationalization but ultimately proved fruitless. The British considered military action against Iran (prefiguring their action during the Suez crisis in 1956) but were dissuaded by the United States. Instead they sought redress at the UN and organized a blockade to prevent Iran exporting oil, but the British secret services also looked for ways to destabilize Mosaddeq, and if possible remove him from office. This included working through numerous Iranian politicians and others acting as proxies and persuading the US government to pursue the same objective. The main US concern was not oil but that Mosaddeq was too dependent on the Soviet-aligned Tudeh party and could be the vehicle for a Soviet takeover in Iran.

After Mosaddeq forced the British embassy in Tehran to close in October 1952, breaking off diplomatic relations, the US government became the prime mover in the efforts to remove him. Meanwhile, deprived of oil income by the British-led embargo, yet still liable for the wage and infrastructure costs of the oil industry, Mosaddeq was running into problems. Some of his previous supporters, including a key political cleric, Ayatollah Kashani, left his governing coalition. In the summer of 1953 the US and British secret services saw their opportunity and organized a coup. The first attempt on the night of August 15–16 failed, because Mosaddeq's supporters were forewarned by Tudeh sympathizers within the army. The Shah, fearing the worst, fled the country. There is some uncertainty and controversy about what happened next, but on August 19, after more unrest (including demonstrations in favor of a republic) a further coup attempt removed Mosaddeq from power (he lived under house arrest until his death in 1967). The Shah returned on August 22, initiating a period of personal rule and repression that ended only with the revolution of 1979.

The removal of Mosaddeq was a central event in the politics of Iran in the twentieth century, and years later was still very much alive in the political memory of Iranians, but its significance was different for different Iranians, according to whether they had leftist or monarchist, or clerical sympathies, and to some extent, whether they lived in Iran or in exile. The events of 1953 were a blow to liberal and democratic politics in Iran; some Iranians, especially younger people, concluded thereafter that more extreme political solutions were necessary. The coup was also a blow to the left in Iran, from which it never really recovered. The Tudeh party was all but destroyed by the Shah's secret police (SAVAK) in the years that followed. Although the involvement of Britain and the United States in Mosaddeq's removal was not revealed for many years (the British government had still, at the time of writing, sixty years later, not formally admitted it), most Iranians soon assumed that those foreign governments had been instrumental in Mosaddeq's fall and the Shah's reinstatement, reconfirming deep-rooted resentment at foreign interference in Iran. For many Iranians, the Shah never really escaped from under the shadow of 1953; they regarded him as an American puppet. This was not entirely fair, especially in the first half of the 1970s. But all these factors were significant in contributing to the revolution of 1979.

What was the White Revolution?

Mosaddeq's government had not been focused solely on oil nationalization. He had also aimed at reforms to limit the power of the monarchy, to introduce welfare provisions and improve health services. In many ways he was seeking to fulfill neglected elements of the constitutionalist program from earlier in the century. But his government had also begun to explore options for land reform.

Agriculture in Iran before the 1960s still followed an ancient pattern. There were complex local variations, but, broadly, agriculture was controlled by a relatively small number of landlords, many of whom belonged to what were popularly known as the "thousand families"— wealthy, conservative, politically influential, often aristocratic and western-educated (though the clergy also were major landowners). Typically, peasants farmed the land on a sharecropping basis, and the landlord took the majority of the produce as rent. The general view was that these landholding arrangements kept the rural population (still a majority of Iran's people) in downtrodden, primitive conditions, made absentee landlords too powerful economically and politically, and kept agricultural production low. The Shah's apparent acquiescence to the traditional arrangements made him and the country appear backward and reactionary (notably by comparison with Egypt, where Nasser's government pursued ambitious land-reform measures from 1952), and pressure for change from progressive-minded Iranians grew through the latter part of the 1950s. At the beginning of the 1960s the new Kennedy administration in the United States added to that pressure, prodding the Shah to take land reform more seriously.

The government's initial proposals for land reform stalled, so in 1962 the Shah brought forward a new Land Reform Act, which he then (in January 1963) presented for a national referendum as part of a six-point plan he called the "White Revolution." The other five points were privatization of state factories, nationalization of forests, female suffrage, profit sharing for workers, and a literacy corps of young educated people who were to go into rural areas to teach reading and writing at primary level; but the program later incorporated a plethora of other measures. The term "White Revolution" reflected the Shah's desire to preempt and avoid a Marxist or Red revolution by improving the people's material living conditions. The referendum approved the measures by a large margin, but it was a revolution from the top: paternalistic in spirit and (with the partial exception of voting rights for women) making little change to the prevailing moribund conditions of Iranian politics.

Land reform was the dominant element in the White Revolution package. The idea was that former sharecroppers would be allowed to buy the land they farmed at preferential rates, with soft loans. For the Shah, the policy had two main objectives, and a number of other subordinate ones. He hoped to create a class of peasant supporters loyal to the monarchy (splitting them from their traditional relationship with the clergy), but also to encourage movement of surplus rural population to the cities to become workers in new industries as part of the planned industrialization of the economy. In addition, the Shah and his planners hoped to modernize and increase agricultural production, and to weaken and marginalize the landlord class, some of whom had Anglophile tendencies and had a diffident attitude to Pahlavi rule.

Implementation exposed a number of weaknesses and contradictions in the land-reform plan. Landlords could keep one village each, but some were able to evade the reform law, for example, by giving their property to relatives or by creating mechanized farms, which were exempt. About two million peasants became landowners in their own right for the first time, and some could make good livings for themselves. But for many more, their landholdings were too small for subsistence, and there were large numbers of agricultural laborers who, because they had not had cultivation rights as sharecroppers before the reform, were left out of the redistribution altogether. Because the reform was accompanied by a general push for the mechanization of agriculture, there was suddenly less work for these laborers anyway. The net result (augmented by generally accelerating population growth) was rural unemployment and a big movement of people from the villages to the cities, especially Tehran, in search of jobs. It has been suggested that the rate of internal migration reached 8 percent per year in 1972–1973, and by 1976 Tehran had swollen to become a city of 4.5 million people.

The reform met the aim of urbanization—perhaps even more dramatically than intended. It also weakened the landowning class; but it failed to create a class of peasants loyal to the Shah. They were not especially grateful to the Shah (perhaps, as elsewhere, they simply regarded the land as theirs anyway) and they remained close to the clerics. They resented the greater state involvement in rural affairs (the literacy corps initiative was also a failure for the most part) and the disruption caused by land reform. This disruption was often severe. Landlords or their local bailiffs had been the ones to manage vital communal necessities like the repair of irrigation works and the marketing of produce. In addition, in the later 1960s and into the 1970s, the government imported staple foods in large quantities to keep food prices low and feed the urban workers. Low food prices depressed the rural economy generally.

Despite efforts toward mechanization and greater efficiency, agricultural production was slow to grow. The White Revolution had dramatic effects, but many of those effects were unintended.

How did the nature of Mohammad Reza Shah's rule change in the 1970s?

Mohammad Reza Shah did not have his father's single-minded, rather brutal self-confidence. He was intelligent, but sometimes aloof and awkward socially. Having been educated in Switzerland from the age of eleven, he was just as at home in Europe as in Iran, but one could also say that he was ill at ease in either. The early years of his reign were traumatic and often humiliating; from the abdication of his father, the Allied occupation, the failure of his first marriage in 1945, an assassination attempt in 1949 that he nearly did not survive, the roller-coaster of the 1953 coup episode (which could easily have destroyed the monarchy), to the divorce from his beloved second wife, Soraya, in 1958.

But he overcame the disturbances and riots around the introduction of the White Revolution program in 1963 (despite the eventual referendum in favor, a downturn in the economic cycle had contributed to unemployment and a resurgence of political dissent)—helped by tough and timely action against them by his prime minister, Asadollah Alam. Repression of dissent by SAVAK became harsher and more comprehensive. Through the latter part of the 1960s the Iranian economy grew, strengthened by investment from the higher share of oil revenues achieved in the aftermath of 1953. Then at the beginning of the 1970s the Shah was able to strengthen his control of oil production, and through negotiation with other members of the oil cartel, OPEC (Organisation of Oil Exporting Countries), to agree measures that quadrupled the oil price (in 1973).

Having ruled in the 1940s and 1950s, as he himself had seen it, with the permission of the United States and United Kingdom, the Shah now began to come out of his shell. A symbol of this was the celebration held in 1971 at Persepolis for 2,500 years of monarchy in Iran. It was a huge, expensive, extravagant event, to which large numbers of foreign heads of state and their representatives were invited. It stressed the monarchy's connections back to the glories of pre-Islamic Iran, sidelining the Islamic heritage that was central to most Iranians' ideas of themselves. It portrayed Iran as an ancient civilization central to world history, which had again reached a position of power and confidence, and was quite successful in delivering that message—but mainly to foreigners. In the 1960s he had published a book, *Mission for My Country*, in which he had portrayed himself as a father to his wayward, rather backward people. He wrote of his hope that they would eventually be able, with his guidance, to reach a higher level of political self-governance (along the lines of western models) for which they were unfortunately not yet ready. In the 1970s he felt able to set aside that posture, and there was little talk of a transition to democracy anymore.

As revenue from oil boomed, the Shah gave interviews to western journalists in which he showed little sympathy for the economic trauma the rapid oil price rises had caused in Europe and the United States, suggesting that those countries were victims of their own decadence and the laziness of their working populations. Given the history of his father's deposition and his own humiliations, speaking in this way to the British in particular must have held some sweetness for him. Enjoying a new sense of independence, he set aside the pretensions to democratic politics that he had expressed earlier. In 1975 he set up a new single party, Rastakhiz ("resurgence"), abolishing the previous two-party structure. As he did so, he made a speech suggesting that all his people should join Rastakhiz, or leave the country, or be regarded as traitors. Rastakhiz put out its feelers into almost all sectors of society, including the countryside, the clergy, and the bazaar. It seemed to be modeled more on the political arrangements of contemporary communist or former fascist countries than on democratic systems.

But all this, like the economic planning and the White Revolution reforms, was from the top down. Rastakhiz was not a grass-roots organization capable of transmitting popular concerns and demands upward to the Shah; it was designed for enforcing the official line and suppressing dissent. The Shah himself did not mix with ordinary Iranians; fearful of further assassination attempts, he separated himself from them with extensive security precautions. His court was full of rivalries and sycophancy; with few exceptions his courtiers tended to tell him what he wanted to hear and recycle regime propaganda back to him. The Shah lived in a bubble, believing his own notions of an ancient quasi-mystical bond between Shah and people that had little foundation in reality. His greater self-confidence was brittle and ill-founded.

4

THE REVOLUTION OF 1979

Who was Ruhollah Khomeini and how did he come to wield such influence over Iranians?

Ruhollah Musavi Khomeini was born in September 1902 in Khomein, a small town between Tehran and Isfahan. He came from a family that had been clerics for several generations and had lived for a time in India in the early nineteenth century. His father died a year after his birth and his mother in 1918, leaving him an orphan dependent on members of his extended family. He was brought up to be a cleric, training in Soltanabad and later in Qom, but from an early stage Khomeini showed an interest in studies that were not typical for the ulema. He showed special interest in the mystical tradition in Islam, in philosophy and poetry (all subjects that were regarded with suspicion and hostility by many traditional-minded clerics). He also developed strong views on the role of the clergy in politics, disagreeing with the orthodox Shi'a view that the clergy should distance themselves from worldly matters. To what extent he developed these ideas because he was taught by clerics who had atypical ideas themselves, or whether he himself sought them out, is not clear. Probably it was a combination of the two, but it is plain that from an early point he had a clear sense of confidence in his own convictions, and drew the attention of other clerics.

One aspect of the idea of Islamic mysticism Khomeini followed (derived from the thirteenth-century Sufi thinker Ibn 'Arabi) was the notion that an individual could, through meditation, study, and prayer "polish his soul"— in other words, develop himself mentally and spiritually— to become the Perfect Man (*al-Insan al-Kamil*), and thereby a conduit for the mind of God in the world. This seems to have been a model for Khomeini's personal sense of mission.

Khomeini's idea of himself was one factor in his rise to political power, but another necessary condition for it was the social position that the clergy had attained in Iran by the twentieth century (discussed in chapter 2). Traditionally, in many villages and small towns, the mullah was the main authority figure (perhaps along with a landlord and some village elders). Before the twentieth century there was no direct representative of the central government in most such places. Junior mullahs like these were connected with others and with the main Shi'a centers of learning through friendships and patron/client relationships made during their training, but also, most importantly, through their allegiance to a *marja* and money payments to him. These arrangements constituted a hierarchy of communication and subordination not unlike that of the Catholic church in Europe; one could see it as a kind of state in waiting. Ordinary Muslims were accustomed to appealing to mullahs for advice and for legal judgment; it was natural for them to look to the clergy in times of political crisis too. Some traditional clerics would be reluctant to give opinions on political matters; others, like Khomeini, less so.

The ever-increasing presence and influence of the West was a dilemma for the clergy. They were never a homogeneous group and different clerics responded in different ways. But most were suspicious, many were resentful, and some openly hostile. This was partially because western ideas of society and the state subverted the role of the clergy in education and the law, for example. Furthermore, well-informed clerics knew that religion had been eclipsed in many parts of Europe, especially since the French Revolution, by secular thinking; they knew too that some Iranians hostile to the clergy welcomed that secularization as a model. These clerics also felt, like other Iranians, the humiliations imposed by westerners and their governments. Finally, at a lower level, their hostility was rooted in the fact that the West was traditionally regarded as alien and the enemy of Islam.

How to respond to this encroaching influence? Should the clergy simply sit back and watch it happen? Or should it, as a class, set aside its traditional aloofness and work with other political groups to combat the influence? The problem with that strategy, from the standpoint of the clergy in the 1960s, was that the other groups were all, to a greater or lesser extent, contaminated by western thinking, whether the Pahlavi monarchy or the secular intellectuals (let alone the communists). In the time of the constitutional revolution, and again in the early months of Mosaddeq's prime ministership, important clerics had allied themselves with the secular liberals, only for the relationship to go sour.

But the clergy's relationship with the monarchy had also gone sour in the past; notably in the time of Reza Shah in the 1930s. In 1963 it went wrong again. After 1953 the clergy were broadly in support of the monarchy, in line with the traditional clerical position and the views of the dominant marja, Ayatollah Seyyed Hosein Borujerdi. But Borujerdi and most other clerics strongly disapproved of the Shah's land-reform plans. When Borujerdi died in 1961 there was a vacuum for a time at the top of the clerical hierarchy.

Khomeini came to the fore and was gradually accepted as an Ayatollah in the following months, but others (notably Mohsen al-Hakim and later Abol Qasem al-Khoei in Najaf) were more respected as marjas.

While Borujerdi was alive, Khomeini obeyed his order not to engage openly and actively in politics. But his death coincided with the growing controversy over land reform and the Shah's White Revolution program. Khomeini avoided pronouncements on land reform, but made trenchant criticisms of the Shah's other policies, including female suffrage and his relations with the United States and Israel. He was arrested several times but refused to shut up or moderate his statements. His forthright speeches made him more and more popular, articulating opposition to the Shah in a way no one else seemed capable of doing at the time. Eventually (in 1964) the Shah sent him into exile. Initially he lived in Turkey, later in Iraq.

While in Iraq, his political views matured. Having opposed the Shah's policies, he came to reject the idea of monarchy altogether, advocating instead the establishment of an Islamic Republic, according to the principle of *velayat-e faqih*. This is a difficult term to translate simply. Velayat means deputyship or guardianship, the authority of someone who is allowed to exercise power because the real authority figure is absent. A faqih is a cleric: a jurist, someone learned in *fiqh*—religious law, the shari'a. So velayat-e faqih is sometimes translated as "guardianship of the jurist," but essentially it means the right of the clergy to govern. Khomeini argued that real authority to rule belonged to God, or to the Hidden Emam, guided by God. In the Emam's absence the clergy—or rather one supreme cleric, a marja—had this right because (1) someone had to rule; (2) human conduct had to be governed by shari'a law; therefore (3) the clergy, as those trained in the shari'a, were logically the only ones suitable.

Khomeini's arguments were not widely accepted, or even widely known before 1979. Until the success of the revolution in that year his only followers were his own former students; clerics like Hosein-Ali Montazeri, Morteza Motahhari, and Mohammad Beheshti.

Later on, in 1978, coming under pressure from the Iraqi government, Khomeini moved from Iraq to Paris.

What were the causes of the revolution of 1979?

Unlike a coup or some other lesser event that brings political change, a revolution implies change of greater magnitude, involving the replacement of not just individuals but whole political and social classes; of not just policies or political programs but whole systems of government, ideologies, constitutions, and public doctrines; of arrangements not just of two or three or five years' duration but leading to change that lasts generations, perhaps with global implications.

The Iranian revolution of 1979 bears comparison with the French revolution of 1789 and the Russian revolution of 1917, according to such criteria. But an event of that importance, on that scale, tends not to have a simple origin or cause; the complexity of its origins usually produces controversy and dispute in its interpretation.

There were several different social and political groups involved in the revolution of 1979, and each had their own discrete motivation. Part of the story of the revolution is the way that those groups came together against the Shah, under the leadership of Khomeini. But after the revolution the interests of those groups diverged again, and some of them felt betrayed by the Islamic Republic. So today there are several different, conflicting and deeply held interpretations of why and how the revolution happened. A balanced view would say that most of these accounts held some truth, and that the revolution arose from a multiplicity of causes.

One plain cause of the revolution was the Shah's long-standing failure to provide an outlet for the political aspirations of his people. The older generation had adjusted wearily and reluctantly to this after 1953, but by the 1970s a new generation had come forward, some of them influenced by the radical student activism and enthusiasm for violent revolutionary action that had been fashionable in Europe and elsewhere in the 1960s. One key group in the revolution was that of secular leftist students, some more radical than others. Others included older leftists, Tudeh sympathizers, and supporters of Mosaddeq's National Front. A substantial number of educated Iranians still aspired to constitutionalism and the principles of the constitution of 1906.

Another factor was the alienation of the clergy from the Shah. Khomeini was the most extreme example, but other clergy were resentful too of the Shah's westernizing, secular reforms, his emphasis on the monarchy's roots in pre-Islamic Iran, and the burgeoning western-style materialism apparent in Iran's cities. Closely allied with the clergy, as ever, were the bazaar merchants and artisans, who disliked changes in patterns of economic activity that pushed their traditional role at the center of the economy to the margin, whether it be new supermarkets in the suburbs or imported foodstuffs. Many of these groups, but especially perhaps the bazaaris, were disturbed by the introduction of Rastakhiz. Previously many had thought that the regime would leave them alone if they stayed quiet and pursued their own economic business, but Rastakhiz sounded as though it would intervene down to the lowest level in the lives of ordinary people; one signal of this was the arrest of large numbers of bazaaris for alleged profiteering as inflation rose in 1976–1977 (a parallel with events of 1905–1906). In addition to the religious students and bazaaris most directly connected with the clergy, there was a group with both religious and constitutionalist sympathies (the Freedom Movement—small but significant), and two radical student groups: one that attempted to fuse both Islam and Marxism—the Mojahedin-e Khalq Organisation (MKO) and another that was more straightforwardly leftist, the Fedayan-e Khalq.

Another set of factors were the economic and social conditions in the period before the revolution. The social upheaval and dislocation caused by land reform brought large numbers of poor, ill-educated young men to Tehran in search of work. After the boom of the early and mid-1970s the economy went into a downturn in 1976–1977; there was downward pressure on wages and some additional unemployment, at a time when prices and rents were still rising. For the most part, evidence indicates that the urban poor were not much involved in the early stages of the revolution, but became more important in the autumn of 1978 when strikes began to cripple the economy and the government. The economic downturn made all social classes feel insecure and more critical of the government; one downside of the Shah's personal rule and one-party state was that there was no one else to blame when things began to go wrong.

There were other contributory causes, some of them already mentioned: the Shah's remoteness from his people, and his expectation that Marxism or the actions of the US or British governments were the main threats to his rule. He was looking the wrong way. Another, perhaps, was the Shah's illness—as the 1970s drew on he was increasingly ill from a form of leukemia (from which he eventually died, in exile, in 1980).

But when all that is said, a part of the explanation remains beyond the reach of this kind of analysis, because only a narrative account that explains the succession of events and responses to them can explain the way that the Shah lost power and the revolution became unstoppable.

Why was the revolution so marked by anti-western rhetoric?

As with the revolution itself, a variety of different attitudes and motivations flowed into a general anti-western stream. Most important was the deep resentment at past foreign interference in Iran, from the humiliations and loss of territory in the nineteenth century to the breaches of Iranian neutrality and sovereignty in the two world wars, and then, to cap it all, the coup of 1953. Paradoxically, many if not most Iranians felt an affinity and even admiration for the people of western countries (especially the United States), and it was common at the time, and has been since, for revolutionaries to say that it was not the people of western countries that were the object of their hostility, but the governments of those countries. Part of this complex feeling was a humiliating disappointment. Many educated Iranians felt let down by the West—especially the United States. They felt that these countries should have been Iran's friends and had repeatedly presented themselves as such, only to betray the trust that Iranians put in them.

For more conservative Iranians less well acquainted with western education or western ideas, the actual experience of western-style advertising, films, and clothing that were thrust at them in TV media and in the streets was off-putting and crassly insensitive to Iran's religious and cultural traditions. Many people felt disoriented and affronted by the eruption of brash American advertising and media in particular. There were large numbers of foreign expatriates in Iran, especially Americans (as many as fifty thousand by the end of the 1970s) and although there were many exceptions, many Iranians felt some Americans behaved in an arrogant and inconsiderate way. They felt to some extent like strangers in their own country, especially in Tehran. Khomeini himself suggested in a speech in 1979 (after the revolution, but with the prerevolution situation in mind) that the vaunted freedoms of the West were being forced on Iranians only the better to subject them to foreign control:

> *These people who want freedom, who want our youth to be free ... What freedom do they want? ... they want the gambling casinos to remain freely open, the bars to be freely open, they want the fleshpots to remain freely open, they want heroin addicts to be free, opium addicts to be free. ... this is something by which they want to emasculate our youth, who could stand up to them ... These pseudodemocrats who proclaim that they should be free, that under no circumstances should anything be banned, are inspired by the superpowers, who want to plunder us and keep our youth indifferent.*

A further point about Tehran in the 1970s was anxiety and resentment about sex. The city had filled up with young men; some students, a larger number looking for paid work. Many of them were from conservative rural or provincial urban families. Some were unemployed; some found poorly paid jobs; most of them lived in poor conditions in the south of the city, where women wore the chador. But in the north of the city they could see young women walking around unchaperoned, wearing (to them) provocative and revealing western fashions. Wealth, immodesty, and western influences seemed to go together. They could also see images of women in advertising and on racy billboards for films outside cinemas. All this was tantalizing, out of reach. It reminded them of their seemingly hopeless inferiority. They could not afford to marry and set up a home, and their resentment was deepened by the strictures of their religious upbringing, and the alien foreignness of the images and fashions. Frustrated desire added to social tension and the resentment of western influences.

These complex attitudes were augmented and given form, especially among the leftist students and the younger generation, by the imported rhetoric of 1960s student radicalism, of anti-imperialism, the anti–Vietnam War movement, and so forth. But many younger Iranians who might have turned to leftism in an earlier generation, in the 1970s turned to Islam as the core of an authentic Iranian identity.

Why did Iran turn away from western, secular models of development toward political Islam?

Iranians have a strong tradition of respect for learning, education, and intellectual endeavor, reflecting their civilization's ancient roots, and writers and thinkers have had a political influence and a status as role models that is not readily translatable into an Anglo-Saxon context. Earlier in the twentieth century, as elsewhere in the Middle East, intellectuals with secular nationalist and constitutionalist attitudes who saw progress in terms of a western model were the leaders in debates on politics and the role of Iran in the world; people like Ahmad Kasravi, Hasan Taqizadeh, and Mohammad Ali Jamalzadeh. In the 1940s some who had shared those views turned more toward communism—one can take Sadegh Hedayat as an example of that trend.

Part of the significance of 1953 was that it led to a further reorientation of attitudes among educated Iranians, writers, and intellectuals. Some of them moved from a position aligned with Tudeh and broadly in sympathy with communism toward a view that laid renewed emphasis on Islam as the authentic center of Iranian identity (there is, of course, an irony in the fact that, as with the idea of nationalism earlier, the concept of authenticity itself betrayed the influence of western thinkers of the same period like Jean-Paul Sartre and Albert Camus). Among these, two names stand out: Jalal Al-e Ahmad and Ali Shariati.

Like many other Iranian intellectuals, Jalal Al-e Ahmad was born into a religious family (in 1923) but turned away from religion. In the 1940s he was close to the leftist thinker and politician Khalil Maleki, but having been a strong supporter of Mosaddeq, he pulled away from politics after 1953. He remained strongly political in much of his work, while withholding support from any particular party or group. His most famous work was first published in 1962—*Gharbzadegi*, which can be translated as "Westoxication" or "West-strickenness." Al-e Ahmad had not coined the term, but he developed it further than anyone else—after the revolution it became one of the standard terms of revolutionary politics. Al-e Ahmad's intention with it was not to attack the West or western ideas as such, at least not directly, but rather the way in which western influences had been accepted and advocated (often without being properly understood), producing people and a culture that were neither genuinely Iranian nor exactly western.

Above all, Al-e Ahmad wanted Iranian cultural life to be *genuine*, not bogus or emptily imitative. As time went on, he left behind the anticlericalism of Kasravi, Hedayat, and the Marxists, and turned back to Iranian Shi'ism as the central, authentic identity of Iran. He supported Khomeini's attacks on the Shah in the early 1960s. To many Iranians he was a hero; the archetype of the politically committed intellectual, complete with beret and tobacco-stained moustache.

Ali Shariati was younger (born in 1933), and even more influential among the young revolutionaries of the 1970s. He too came from a clerical family; his own father had been influential in a group that tried to blend socialist and Islamic ideas in the 1950s. Shariati also had been a strong supporter of Mosaddeq, but had also been disillusioned, coming to believe that democratic principles were not strong enough to overcome tyranny in a country like Iran. He studied sociology in Paris on a government scholarship and then taught in Mashhad, where he had been a student himself. He was a charismatic teacher and gained a following both there and in Tehran by advocating a new form of revolutionary Islam, that stressed the ideas of social and political justice that underpinned the revelation of Mohammad but was critical (like many of the earlier thinkers) of clerical conservatism, obtuseness, and obsession with the scholastic detail of scriptural texts. Sometimes it is said of Shariati that his views fused Marxism and Islam; this is not the case. Rather he aimed to present Islam anew as an ideology that could bring about revolutionary change: like Marxism but better. He drew particular attention to the example of Hosein as a model for revolutionary leadership and self-sacrifice, and was the originator of the slogan "Every day is Ashura and everywhere is Karbala." Shariati was imprisoned by SAVAK in the 1970s and then held under house arrest. He went to England in 1977 and died there in June the same year, apparently from a heart attack.

These were the ideas that captured the imaginations of many Iranian students and young people in the 1960s and 1970s, and which prepared them to accept Khomeini's leadership. Khomeini himself never endorsed Shariati or Al-e Ahmad or their ideas explicitly (nor denounced them) but his speeches sometimes echoed their language and thinking.

When and how did the Shah lose control of the country?

Some foreign observers noted the economic problems that the Shah ran into in 1977, but few predicted that his government would get into serious difficulties. The Shah visited Washington at the end of that year, and President Carter rewarded him with a speech that hailed his rule in

Iran as an "island of stability" in a troubled region. As a Democratic president trying to reassert the importance of human rights in US foreign policy, Carter had mixed views about Iran. The Shah was an important regional ally (and there is little evidence that Carter applied any direct diplomatic pressure to liberalize), but the human rights record of his regime was poor. From the Shah's point of view, he had always found it easier to get along with Republican presidents, but wanted to do what he could to mollify Carter. He relaxed some of the repressive measures he had applied to stifle dissent, and over the course of 1977 some tentative opposition voices began to speak up again.

In the autumn a series of poetry evenings hosted by the Goethe Institut in Tehran attracted growing numbers of leftist intellectuals and students, and became more political and critical of the Shah's government until they came to an end. At around the same time religious students demonstrated angrily in Qom at the news that Khomeini's son Mostafa had died in Iraq (in Najaf) in suspicious circumstances. These demonstrations were marked by declarations of support for Khomeini and opposition to the Shah. Perhaps in response to this, in January 1978 the government placed a propagandist article in the newspaper *Ettela'at*, saying among other things that Khomeini was not really Iranian, that he had been a British spy, and that he had written indecent poetry. The article caused outrage among Khomeini's followers, and new demonstrations in Qom. But this time the authorities intervened and fired on the demonstrators with live ammunition, causing several deaths.

This set in train a phenomenon that was crucial for the growth of the revolutionary movement. It was traditional after a death to wait for forty days and then commemorate the deceased with a day of mourning (called *arba'in* in Arabic or *chelom* in Persian) —a practice familiar to all

Iranians irrespective of their politics. Forty days after the Qom shootings there were renewed demonstrations in mourning for those killed in Qom—not just there but in several other cities, and especially in Tabriz, which had been the home town of at least one of those who had died in January. There were more confrontations with police in Tabriz, and more shootings, and so further demonstrations after another forty days. And so it went on, with the demonstrations growing in size each time. At this stage, some clerics, demonstrators, and others were calling for reforms, and the proper implementation of the constitution of 1906 (also the relaxation of censorship and the release of political prisoners); not all supported Khomeini's intransigent demand for the Shah to be removed. But as time went on, more and more of the opposition aligned themselves with Khomeini, whose regular speeches and statements reached the people by means of cassette tapes, fax machines, and the BBC World Service (especially after he moved to Paris in October 1978). There was little violence against persons, but in several cities buildings associated with the regime or with western influences, like police stations, banks, or cinemas, were attacked and sometimes sacked. In early summer some clerics called for a pause, in order to avoid further bloodshed, and so the demonstrations stopped for a time.

Nonetheless, another event maintained the tension—on August 19 there was a fire started by arson at the Rex cinema in Abadan, in the southwest, killing 370 people. Since then it has been demonstrated that the fire was started by opposition activists associated with radical clerics, which was what the government said at the time—but such was the strength of feeling against the regime in the summer of 1978 that it was widely assumed that the Shah's government had started the fire, in order to discredit the religious opposition.

Ramadan fell in August that year, and there were renewed demonstrations at the end of Ramadan, in early September. The first of these was an impromptu march on September 4 that began in the northern part of Tehran after a prayer meeting to mark the end of Ramadan. With an estimated number of participants between two hundred thousand and five hundred thousand, it was much larger than those that had gone before, by a large margin. It was mainly peaceful, but another demonstration on September 7 took on a darker mood after security forces tried to break up the crowd with tear gas.

A further demonstration was organized for September 8, but, unknown to many of the participants, martial law was declared overnight, and the demonstrators were met by armed troops. At Jaleh Square in south Tehran the soldiers fired on the crowd, killing about eighty people and wounding many more, but (as with the Rex cinema fire) no one believed the government's statements to that effect, and many believed that thousands had been killed.

This sequence of events in early September seems finally to have made the Shah (and the western governments who supported him) realize that his throne was in serious danger, but it seems also to have been the crucial point at which a critical mass of Iranians decided that the Shah had gone too far and was no longer fit to rule. He kept trying, appointing and firing new ministers, making promises about liberalization and free elections, and so on, but his announcements fell on deaf ears. As the autumn went on, an intensifying crescendo of strike actions delivered a final and decisive series of blows to the regime. The strikes were partly about poor working conditions and low wages, but took on the mood and grievances of the demonstrations also. With the security forces intact, the Shah's government could perhaps have ridden out the demonstrations, enormous though they had grown. But the strikes, especially in the oil industry, struck at tax revenue, the basis of the government's power, and there was no remedy for them.

By the end of the year, the police hardly dared show their faces in the streets, law and order was breaking down in many of the cities, and in some places local committees were taking over food and fuel distribution (often based in mosques) and neighborhood policing. Over the autumn opposition politicians from the National Front and the Freedom party visited Khomeini (in Paris) and publicly accepted his leadership (as did other opposition elements). In December there were a series of huge demonstrations around the annual Ashura commemorations, attended by more than a million people each time, at which crowds called for an Islamic Republic and shouted "Death to the Shah." Around this time the Shah finally decided to accept defeat, and he left the country on January 16. Ordinary Iranians celebrated joyously in the streets. On February 1 Khomeini returned to Tehran from exile, to be welcomed by a crowd that has been estimated at three million.

How did Khomeini consolidate his and his followers' grip on power after his return from exile on February 1, 1979?

Before the Shah left in January 1979, he appointed a new prime minister, Shapur Bakhtiar, who had previously had close associations with the National Front, in the hope that Bakhtiar could be a compromise figure between the monarchy and the revolutionary movement. But Bakhtiar's short-lived government was tainted by the fact that the Shah had appointed him, and by further deaths at demonstrations in the latter part of January. When Khomeini returned from France, Bakhtiar's days as prime minister were numbered. Officials and military officers that had served under the Shah were falling over each other to make deals with the new regime and make themselves safe, if possible. Khomeini appointed his own prime minister, Mehdi Bazargan (head of the Freedom Movement), on February 5, and on February 9–10 a confrontation between pro-Khomeini air force technicians and loyalist army personnel at Doshan Tappeh air base (to the east of the city center of Tehran) escalated into a gun battle, drawing in revolutionary fighters (including many MKO fighters) from the outside, and army reinforcements. But such were the crowds and the spontaneous mobilization against the army on the streets that the troops and tanks were for the most part unable to get through.

On the morning of February 11 senior army commanders gathered together, and after extended discussions agreed the situation was hopeless. They decided effectively to withdraw from the struggle, by making a declaration of so-called neutrality. Bakhtiar received the news with dismay, but there was nothing he could do. He went into hiding, and later managed to leave the country in secret and go into exile. Khomeini and Bazargan's provisional government were left in control. The last obstacle to the full success of the revolution had given way.

Khomeini and his fellow clerics were not natural revolutionaries. As a class the ulema tended to be traditionalist and conservative. Khomeini wanted to avoid anarchy, and was acutely aware that despite his popularity he had no organized paramilitary force to back his position, unlike the MKO and some other leftist groups. Remembering the clergy's previous failed ventures into politics, he needed to turn his unprecedented popularity into lasting political authority for himself and his successors. He may not, at the outset, have envisaged as extended a role for clerical power as eventually took shape in practice (initially he went to live in Qom rather than stay in Tehran). The arrangement by which Bazargan ran the government as prime minister could have meant a more distant, presiding role for

Khomeini. But from the start it became clear that Khomeini and his closest advisers (notably Ayatollah Beheshti) were not going to allow themselves to be sidelined. Others who had supported the revolution against the Shah (notably the leftists) hoped or expected precisely that the clergy, traditionalist and unworldly in politics, could be shouldered aside and that they could take real power for themselves. They were to be disappointed.

Bazargan quickly discovered that significant parts of his authority as head of the government were subverted or usurped by new, revolutionary bodies owing allegiance to Khomeini. There were revolutionary courts, headed by clerical judges, busy expropriating and in some cases executing people associated with the previous regime. Revolutionary committees (*komiteh*) continued to run local affairs; armed members made arrests and enforced shari'a law. On May 5, Khomeini set up the Revolutionary Guard Corps (Sepah-e Pasdaran) as guardians of the revolution against internal and external threats. Even within Bazargan's theoretical remit, Khomeini and his advisors appointed representatives to each government ministry and army unit. These representatives operated a little bit like Soviet commissars. Despite a referendum at the end of March that approved the establishment of an Islamic Republic by a majority of 98.2 percent, there were nonetheless threats to the new government. On May 1 Khomeini's friend and devoted follower Morteza Motahhari was assassinated. A secessionist insurrection in Iranian Kurdestan broke out over the spring and summer as Kurds realized that the Shah's overthrow was not going to bring them the regional autonomy they had hoped for (pro-autonomy movements also surfaced in Khuzestan, Baluchestan, and among the Turkmen in the northeast). Over the summer thugs and paramilitaries associated with the revolutionary committees broke into several offices of newspapers and political organizations not aligned with Khomeini and his followers, beginning the imposition of a new era of censorship. There was a fluidity and uncertainty in politics that Khomeini and his people regarded as dangerous, encouraging them to take greater control.

For most of 1979 political debate centered on the form that the new constitution would take. Initially it looked as though a relatively moderate draft constitution, prepared by politicians from the Freedom Movement close to Bazargan, would be put into effect. But as the procedures for preparation of the constitution went ahead (an Assembly of Experts, mainly clerics, was elected in August and debated the constitution for most of September and October) a constitution with a much more strongly Islamic character emerged, based more explicitly on the principle of velayat-e faqih and accordingly with a much stronger role for Khomeini and his future successors as Leader.

Why did the Iranians occupy the US Embassy in November 1979, and why did it take so long to release the hostages?

Like other symbols of a western presence in Iran, embassies had been attacked by demonstrators several times during the revolution. The British embassy had been briefly occupied and partly burned in November 1978 (it happened again in November 1979) and the US embassy had been occupied briefly in February 1979. So when a group of students broke into the US embassy again on November 4, 1979, taking hostage sixty-six US diplomats and marines (six escaped capture, were helped by the British ambassador on to the Canadian embassy, and were able eventually to leave the country, as somewhat misrepresented in the 2012 film *Argo*), most people assumed that the occupation would be a short protest, and the students would soon withdraw again.

Some have suggested since that time that the students' occupation of the embassy was a deliberate, premeditated act designed by Khomeini himself or by his close associates, as a blow to the United States, or to destabilize their opponents, or for some other purpose. There is no direct evidence to support this. That is not to say it cannot be true, but there is some evidence that Khomeini initially dismissed the break-in as unimportant and was inclined to have the students removed. At any rate, early on November 5 he made a statement supporting the students and alleging that the embassy had been a "nest of spies." Others close to Khomeini made similar statements, and the following day Bazargan, who had called for the hostages' release, resigned. What had happened?

As the debate on the constitution had matured over the two previous months, liberals like Bazargan, and leftists and many of the others in the broad stream that had supported the revolution (including in particular a moderate cleric, Ayatollah Shariatmadari), came to realize that the new form the constitution was taking gave Khomeini and his supporters overwhelming power in the new republic— arguably, more than the Shah had enjoyed. The strongly pro-Khomeini composition of the Assembly of Experts prevented them from opposing these developments effectively there. But there was to be a referendum on the constitution before it entered into force. Through October it began to look as though the disparate groups unhappy with the constitution might combine to oppose it ahead of the referendum.

On October 22 it became known that the Carter administration had allowed the Shah into the United States for medical treatment. From that point onward Khomeini made speeches attacking the United States and denouncing the Shah, with increasing intensity. In the middle of this, on November 1, Bazargan went with Ebrahim Yazdi, his foreign minister, to Algiers to meet the US national security adviser, Zbigniew Brzezinski (with Khomeini's knowledge). They discussed tentative steps toward an improvement of Iran-US relations, and the possible resumption of the sale of spare parts for the weapon systems the Shah had bought over the previous decade. But back in Tehran the coincidence with the Shah's arrival looked suspicious, and in the febrile atmosphere of revolutionary politics it was interpreted as the beginnings of a plot to bring about a coup to end the revolution, along the lines of 1953. This is what the students thought they were forestalling by the occupation of the embassy. Their prime demand was that the United States should send the Shah back to Iran to face a revolutionary court.

By supporting the students and their occupation, Khomeini captured the initiative, destabilized his opponents, and re-radicalized the revolution. The hostage crisis became the central issue; opposition to the occupation could be interpreted as suspicious collusion with the revolution's enemies. The leftists, eager for any kind of anti-Americanism, enthusiastically supported it, fixing a gulf between themselves and liberals like Bazargan. Any potential for an alliance against the constitution was shattered. The debates on the constitution in the Assembly of Experts concluded within a couple of weeks, and it was approved by an overwhelming majority at the beginning of December.

Khomeini had got what he wanted. A year later, the students' religious guide, Mohammad Musavi-Khoeniha, expressed it succinctly in a statement in Parliament (the Majles):

> We have reaped the fruits of our undertaking. We defeated the attempt by the "liberals" to take control of the machinery of state. We forced Mr. Bazargan's

government to resign. The tree of revolution has grown and gained in strength. We have demonstrated both to our own people and to international opinion that we have the weapons not only to resist but also to defeat the all-powerful United States, which believed it held Iran in the palm of its hand.

Various negotiations were begun at various stages between different sets of people to bring about the hostages' release, but they repeatedly ran into the sand or otherwise failed. Thirteen of the hostages were released in mid-November, supposedly as a goodwill gesture (they were women and African Americans—another hostage was released later because he was ill). Some progress was made early in 1980 through UN mediation, but was then undercut by an announcement from Khomeini that nothing could be done until the new Parliament was elected in May.

In April 1980 the Carter administration took matters into their own hands and tried to rescue the hostages (encouraged by the startling rescue of hijacked hostages by Israeli special forces at Entebbe in 1976). But the attempt was a failure. The mission had to be aborted when several helicopters dropped out due to mechanical failure, and then, as they withdrew, a helicopter collided with a C-130 tanker aircraft and both disappeared in a ball of flame. Eight US servicemen died. The failure of the rescue mission was a further bitter humiliation for the US government.

The students' persistent demand that the Shah be returned to Iran was an obstacle to the hostages' release, but that obstacle was removed when the Shah finally died, in Egypt, on July 27, 1980. On September 22 Iraq invaded Iran and the isolation caused by Iran's retention of the hostages, which previously perhaps had been a form of revolutionary self-indulgence, became a dangerous and potentially fatal liability. It is clear that the Iranians thereafter negotiated toward the hostages' release with greater seriousness. But there was a further delay, and some have suggested this was because Ronald Reagan's supporters in the presidential election campaign made a secret agreement with the Iranians to hold the hostages' release until after Reagan had taken office, in January 1981; in return for vital weapons spares. There is no proof; if the suggestions are true, the deal was breathtakingly cynical. But the fifty-two remaining hostages were eventually released just a few minutes after Reagan's inauguration on January 20, 1981; and some weapons spares were certainly delivered later.

Carter believed that the hostage crisis was the single most important factor that prevented him winning a second presidential term. For a whole generation of Americans, it was the most shameful foreign policy failure after Vietnam, and its lingering effect poisoned US-Iran relations for many years to come.

5

THE IRAN-IRAQ WAR (1980–1988), RAFSANJANI, KHATAMI, RECONSTRUCTION, AND REFORM

What or who was primarily responsible for the outbreak of the Iran-Iraq war?

Various causes have been presented to explain the origin of the Iran-Iraq war, including deep-seated antagonism between Iranians and Arabs, and the efforts of the Iranian revolutionary government to export the Islamic revolution to Iraq in 1979–1980. But the war began with Iraq's armed forces invading Iranian territory in September 1980, and the prime cause of the invasion was that the Iraqi president, Saddam Hussein, thought he saw an opportunity. Saddam was politically a secular nationalist but came from a Sunni background.

In the Shah's time there had been serious problems between Iraq and Iran. These had escalated in the 1970s to the point that they nearly came to war in the middle of the decade. One point of contention was over the Shatt al-Arab waterway (Arvand Rud in Persian)—the river running between the confluence of the Tigris and Euphrates rivers and the point where their waters flow into the Persian Gulf. This waterway had been the border between the Ottoman Empire and Iran for centuries before the First World War, but the question of whether the border ran along one bank or the other, or through the middle of it, had for most of that time not been a significant problem. The discovery of oil, first in Iran and then in Iraq, changed that. For both countries the waterway was vital for carrying the oil away for export from the adjacent oilfields. Iraq wanted the border to run along the Iranian bank, signifying that Iran would be allowed to use the waterway only with Iraqi permission. The Iranians argued that the waterway should be shared, with an equal right of access and transit.

The dispute took color also from the prevailing conditions of the Cold War. Iraq was backed by the Soviet Union; Iran under the Shah was a key US ally. The Shah put pressure on Iraq by sending support, including weapons, to Kurdish separatists within Iraq in 1974–1975. Iranian artillery fired across the border, and at one point the Shah actually sent Iranian troops over the border to help the Kurdish fighters. But rather than escalate further, the two countries opted to negotiate, and in March 1975 reached agreement in Algiers to stop supporting separatists in each other's countries, and to agree that the Shatt al-Arab border (in accordance with precedents set by border settlements elsewhere in the world) would be in the middle of the river, where the flow was fastest—what in international legal terms is called the *Thalweg*.

But Saddam Hussein, who led the Algiers talks for Iraq, left the talks with a grievance—he believed Iraq had negotiated under duress and that the settlement was unfair. In 1979–1980 this sense of grievance was augmented by Iranian propaganda against what they called the godless Baathist regime in Iraq. There were unrest and demonstrations among Iraqi Shi'as sympathetic to the Iranian revolution and Saddam made use of these to help him take power as president in July 1979 (precise figures are not available but Shi'as probably comprised more than half of the Iraqi population). When Saddam had a prominent Shi'a

Ayatollah murdered in prison in April 1980 Iranian propaganda reached a new pitch of intensity.

Saddam knew that the Iranian military was in disorder and below strength after the revolution; many officers had been purged and some executed, and there had been losses of rank-and-file troops to desertion. From his perspective, invasion seemed to bring several real and potential benefits for little risk. As a minimum, he could take territory quickly and trade it in peace negotiations for a better settlement on the Shatt al-Arab (all recent wars in the Middle East had been short, with brisk campaigns followed by a UN-mediated cease-fire). But there was a chance that Arabs in Khuzestan might rise in revolt against the government in Tehran, in which case he might be able to annex an oil-rich slice of that province. Iran's international isolation might make acceptable changes of borders that previously would have been unthinkable. In the prevailing turmoil in Tehran, invasion might even bring about the collapse of the revolutionary government, removing the propaganda irritant and perhaps facilitating even greater gains. In addition, whatever the outcome, he would win the prestige of being a strong leader in the Arab world.

Saddam was proved right, in that his forces were able to take large swathes of valuable territory in Khuzestan quickly after the invasion in September 1980; he succeeded also in making himself better known across the Middle East (and beyond). But all his other calculations proved wrong.

Why did the Iran-Iraq war last so long?

The short answer to this question is oil. Without the revenue from sales of oil and, in Iraq's case, loans on the basis of future oil revenue, neither side would have been able to sustain their war effort for more than eight years.

Although both sides made attacks on tankers transporting each other's oil through the Persian Gulf, and on oil trans-shipment installations, with few exceptions they avoided attacking oil production installations, for fear of retaliation, crippling damage, and fiscal collapse.

A further answer to the question is related but separate: because (at least at the outset) neither side had an arms industry capable of producing the sophisticated weapons necessary to achieve decisive breakthroughs (aircraft, tanks, artillery), and because these had to be imported and, after import, serviced with expensive spare parts, both sides tended to conserve these valuable weapons and use them defensively (typically, as reserves to counterattack enemy breakthroughs). This meant a general reliance on infantry warfare and a reversion to strategic and tactical conditions reminiscent of the period in the early twentieth century before tanks and aircraft permitted the reemergence of mobile, offensive operations in modern warfare—in other words a reversion to conditions similar to those of the First World War in Europe, dominated by trenches, machine guns, mortars, mines, and barbed wire—conditions that strongly favored the defensive. The miserable similarity with the western front was made stronger by the Iranians' use of mass infantry attacks against defensive positions, often with huge losses, and by the Iraqis' use of chemical weapons. Offensives often failed to achieve their objectives, resulting instead in meager gains and bloody stalemate. The Iraqis used chemical weapons extensively; it has been estimated that they alone caused more than fifty thousand Iranian casualties. By mid-war the Iranians had the capability to retaliate in kind, but never did.

In addition, there were missed opportunities to end the war. Saddam made major territorial gains with the initial invasion in September 1980 and took one important city, Khorramshahr, but then the advance of his forces bogged down as more Iranian regular troops arrived at the front, and large numbers of volunteers came forward (being incorporated into Sepah and Basij volunteer militia units). At this point, Saddam would have accepted a cease-fire, but the Iranians were determined to fight on until they had retaken their lost territory. By the spring of 1982, they had succeeded in driving the Iraqis back more or less to the prewar borders, and could have ended the war at that point (since then, many Iranians have with hindsight accepted that it would have been better to do so). There were two main reasons they did not: first, because the Iranian leadership judged (not without reason) that Saddam would continue to be a threat to Iran until he was removed, and, second, because the recent successful offensives had convinced Iranian commanders (especially the enthusiastic Sepah commanders) that they could successfully continue the war into Iraq and topple Saddam's government. They also thought that Shi'as in southern Iraq might rise up in revolt against Saddam. It is sometimes suggested that Khomeini deliberately prolonged the war in order to consolidate the Islamic republic. If so, it was incidental; the predominant motive, seen at the time as an existential necessity, was to remove Saddam.

But this time, the Iranians were the ones to miscalculate. On both sides in the war, soldiers fought harder to defend their own national territory than to occupy the territory of the enemy, and the hoped-for separatist insurrections did not materialize (except in Kurdestan, but different groups of Kurdish separatists were fighting both Iraq and Iran). The Iranians' human wave tactics were less successful from mid-1982 onward, and the flow of volunteers began to subside. But they kept trying. In order to deter further attacks and in attempts to force the Iranians to accept a cease-fire, Saddam spread the war into new theaters by attacking Iranian oil tankers in the Persian Gulf and by attacking Iranian cities with bombs and long-range missiles. The Iranians retaliated in kind. The United States, the Soviet Union, the United Kingdom, and some other countries sent naval vessels to the Persian Gulf to protect shipping operations.

In the land campaigns the Iranians almost cut the road from Baghdad to Basra on more than one occasion, but not quite; they took the Fao peninsula on the Iraqi side of the Shatt al-Arab in 1986, almost sealing Iraq off from the sea, but then the Iraqis retook it in 1988 (it is now known that the United States assisted with satellite intelligence). Decisive victory remained out of reach.

What was the Iran/Contra affair?

By the end of the Iran-Iraq war US policy had shifted to apply more pressure on Iran, on the basis that Iran was the one refusing to accept the cease-fire and therefore was the one primarily responsible for the continuation of the war. But at an earlier stage, the United States had a more flexible approach, at least in secret. Iran/Contra was a covert deal by which the Reagan administration sought to fulfill policies that it was supposed not to be pursuing: supplying the Iranians with weapons and weapons spares (despite a UN arms embargo), passing funds to the Contra rebels in Nicaragua (despite a ruling from the US Congress that this should not be done), and trying to secure the release of US hostages in Lebanon (despite public statements that the administration would not negotiate with hostage takers). The mechanism relied on Israel as an intermediary. Israel delivered the weapons to Iran, and the money paid to Israel by the Iranians for the weapons was passed back to the Contras by the Israelis. The United States sent Israel replacements for the weapons, and Iran used its influence to bring about the release of American hostages being held by pro-Iranian groups in Lebanon (the central figure on the Iranian side of the deal was Hashemi Rafsanjani). These complicated arrangements became public when details of a series of secret meetings between Iranian and US negotiators were leaked to a Lebanese newspaper in November 1986 (the leak came from the Iranian side—a wayward associate of Hosein-Ali Montazeri was responsible, a man called Mehdi Hashemi).

The furor over Iran/Contra in the United States did damage to the Reagan administration, but it was also dangerous politically in Iran. Collusion with the United States (let alone Israel) had been a damning accusation in Iranian revolutionary politics, and had been used to damage several revolutionary politicians (documents from the occupied US embassy, painstakingly reassembled after shredding, had been exploited for this purpose). When the Iran/Contra story became public, the Iranian regime had to admit dealings with the United States, but continued to deny any negotiations with Israel, and eventually Khomeini intervened to stop any further investigation of the affair. As ever, Khomeini's authority trumped other considerations.

On the Israeli side, those involved were quite clear that they judged it was in their country's long-term best interests to have a strategic relationship with Iran. They had been supplying Iran with weapons quite separately from Iran/Contra almost since the beginning of the war, and continued to do so afterward. A further important instance of this relationship was the Iranian/Israeli cooperation over the bombing of the Iraqi nuclear reactor at Osirak in 1981 (Operation Opera/Babylon). Israeli policy was based on the judgment that whatever rhetoric might have emerged from Iran about Israel, Iraq was a much greater threat (Israeli policy toward Iran did not change until after Netanyahu became prime minister in 1996, and particularly after the fall of Saddam in 2003). At various stages the US side also avowed that one of the purposes of their involvement, along with the release of the hostages, was to improve relations with Iran. In particular, both the United States and Israel hoped that they were positioning themselves to reestablish a working relationship with a more moderate Iranian regime once Khomeini had died. To that end, it seemed to make sense to woo those who appeared to be moderates within the Iranian system (especially Rafsanjani).

After the affair became public in November 1986, investigations within the United States about the affair dragged on for months. In polls of US public opinion, Reagan's personal approval rating dropped from 67 percent to 46 percent. Coming after the damage done to Carter's presidency by the hostage crisis, Reagan's experience was hardly an encouragement to future US administrations to reengage with Iran. From the Iranian point of view, the experience showed once again that public statements and positions taken in multilateral fora by western governments could not be taken at face value (a message reinforced by their wider experience of positions taken internationally toward the Iran-Iraq war). Within Iran, the only ones to suffer from its opprobrium were those associated with the leak that revealed it. Mehdi Hashemi was eventually executed, and the episode was a contributory factor in ensuring that Hosein-Ali Montazeri, who had been Khomeini's nominated successor, never ultimately took that role.

Did Iran win or lose the Iran-Iraq war and why was the war so important?

By the spring and summer of 1988 the pressure on Iran to accept a UN-mediated cease-fire and end the war had become irresistible. New sources of oil had come on stream globally at a time when demand had reduced, causing a drop in the oil price, hitting national finances hard at a vulnerable time. Iran had lost most of the military gains made since 1982 and was finding it more and more difficult to buy arms internationally, while Iraq had re-equipped with new aircraft and other weapons from France, the Soviet Union, and others, and had added nerve gases to its arsenal of chemical agents (a long list of countries had assisted Iraq's chemical weapon program, including Germany, Egypt, France, the United Kingdom, Brazil, India, and Singapore, among others). Iraq's arms procurement had been facilitated by large loans from Kuwait, Saudi Arabia, and other Arab states along the southern shore of the Persian Gulf. In July 1987 four hundred Iranians died in a riot in Mecca while on pilgrimage; the Saudis claimed they had been trampled but the Iranians believed they had been machine-gunned. Pressure on Iran in the Persian Gulf had increased, and was demonstrated by the shooting down of a civilian Iranian airliner by a US warship, the USS *Vincennes*, on July 3, 1988 (290 people died, including many children). The incident was the result of a series of errors and misunderstandings, but the Iranians believed it was deliberate, and they interpreted it, along with other evidence, to signify that the United States would go to any lengths and would never allow Iran to win the war. In addition, there had been several incidents in which the Iraqis had used chemical weapons against civilians: at Sardasht in June 1987, at Halabja in March 1988, and against several settlements on the Iranian side of the border in July 1988. The victims at Halabja were Iraqi Kurds living in a border town that had just been taken by Iranian troops— the United States and others, on the basis of Iraqi intelligence, initially tried to claim that the Iranians had carried out the attack. After these incidents it seems the Iranian leadership believed that the Iraqis might use chemical weapons as warheads on Soviet-supplied Scud missiles in mass attacks directed at Iranian cities, with tacit permission from the superpowers.

The overall impression for the Iranians was that they were not just fighting Iraq, but almost the whole world, that their enemies would use any means, however extreme or inhumane (or illegal in the notional terms of international law), and that their own resources to fight on were inadequate and comparatively dwindling. Rafsanjani, who was now the prime figure directing the war at working level and had spent time touring the front line in the early months of 1988, commissioned an assessment from the head of the Sepah of what Iran would need to win the war. Mohsen Rezai responded with a letter in which he wrote "no victories are in sight for the next five years," and that in order to resume offensive operations Iran would need to be able to create 350 new infantry brigades; to buy 2,500 tanks, 3,000 artillery pieces, and 300 aircraft; and to manufacture laser and nuclear weapons. The army would have to double in size, the Sepah would need to be increased seven-fold, and the United States would need to be evicted from the Persian Gulf. Nonetheless, he concluded, "we have to continue the war."

When Khomeini read the letter, he finally accepted that the war had to come to an end. He said the decision was for him like drinking a chalice of poison, but he accepted it as the will of God. Given Khomeini's previous unrelenting advocacy for the war, and his belief that he had been the mouthpiece for God in the world, the poison metaphor may have been no idle hyperbole. His son Ahmad said later that Khomeini was a changed man after July 1988. He fell ill and died less than a year afterward, in June 1989.

Iran accepted the UN cease-fire resolution with a letter to the UN secretary-general on July 17, 1988. Even then, the war did not end immediately; Saddam attempted unsuccessfully to grab some extra territory as bargaining chips.

A full cease-fire finally entered into effect on August 20, and the fighting was over. But there were no peace negotiations and no peace treaty, and both sides retained prisoners of war well into the 1990s.

Many figures have been given for the number of Iranian casualties in the war, but a recent moderate estimate suggests figures of 213,000 killed and 320,000 permanently disabled (many of whom still suffer the lingering effects of chemical weapons). The figures imply an additional large number of injured who made a fuller recovery.

Both sides claimed victory in the war and in a sense both were right, because both had survived the attempts of the other to destroy them. Iran had not succeeded in removing Saddam from power and had been forced reluctantly into the cease-fire. But over the years, for many Iranians, the country's success in resisting both Iraqi aggression and the passive or active hostility of a larger number of neighboring and more distant countries has become a matter of pride, irrespective of their distaste or affinity for the Islamic regime. For the first time in over two hundred years, Iran had asserted its independence and right to self-defense as a sovereign nation, and had upheld it against the odds. In assessing the attitudes of Iranians and the behavior of their government since 1988, it is essential to remember the lessons they drew from the Iran-Iraq war.

When and why did Iran get involved in Lebanon?

There had been a substantial Shi'a population in what is now southern Lebanon for centuries before the Israeli invasion of Lebanon in June 1982, but in common with many other Shi'a communities in the territory of the former Ottoman Empire and elsewhere in the Islamic world, they had been a minority and had tended to be looked down upon by more privileged Sunni Muslim and Christian elites. There had been renewed contacts between the revolutionaries of the Islamic republic and the Lebanese Shi'as in 1979–1981 (Montazeri was an enthusiast for these contacts, and his protégé Mehdi Hashemi was involved), but after the Israeli invasion these were rapidly expanded and ramped up. Large numbers of Sepah personnel were sent to Lebanon, where they helped to train young Shi'a fighters, on the principle of solidarity with Muslims in other countries, which was part of the revolutionary constitution. The main center of the fighters' activity and recruitment was the Bekaa Valley, and the radicalism induced by the past wrongs felt by the Lebanese Shi'a, the dislocation of the Israeli invasion, and the Iranian influence led to the creation of Lebanese Hezbollah in 1982–1983.

Closely associated with Lebanese Hezbollah and the Iranians in Lebanon (though the details have always been hazy) was an organization called Islamic Jihad, a radical Palestinian group that took hostages in Lebanon and carried out several terrorist actions in subsequent years, many of them associated with Imad Mughniyeh, a Lebanese Shi'a who had associated closely with anti-Israeli Palestinian organizations before 1982. When Mughniyeh was killed by a car bomb in Damascus in 2008, he was described as a senior figure in Hezbollah itself (the assassination was widely reported to have been carried out by Mossad, in association with others).

Both Lebanese Hezbollah and Islamic Jihad from the start presented armed opposition to the state of Israel as one of their prime founding commitments. For Iran, the relationship with Lebanese Hezbollah (and, to a lesser extent, Hamas) has been the means by which it has made real its revolutionary commitment to oppose Israel and show support for the Palestinians. That relationship in turn has been an important aspect of Iran's relationship with Syria, because without Syrian cooperation and without Syrian support in parallel for Lebanese Hezbollah, practical support for Lebanese Hezbollah would be much more difficult for the Iranian regime.

Of all the relationships Iran has with Shi'a Muslim communities and groups elsewhere in the Islamic world, the relationship with Hezbollah in Lebanon is the closest. This was reaffirmed by the support given by the Iranians when Israel invaded Lebanon again in 2006. But even this close relationship is not one of control; the Iranians are not the masters and Hezbollah are not the servants. There is an ambiguity, and for the most part Lebanese Hezbollah follow their own interests. On one significant occasion Lebanese Shi'as resisted Iranian pressure, when in the 1990s they rebuffed attempts to make Iran's Supreme Leader Ali Khamenei their sole *marja*. Most of them chose Mohammad Husein Fadlallah instead (a Shi'a cleric of Lebanese descent, who has taken an independent line on the principle of *velayat-e faqih*, for example). As elsewhere in the Middle East, the Iranians have to tread carefully if they are to exert influence, and do so only on sufferance.

What was the significance of the so-called fatwa against Salman Rushdie?

There was a delay between the publication of Rushdie's *Satanic Verses* in September 1988 and Khomeini's infamous statement (in strict terms of Islamic practice, it was in fact a *hokm*, or religious order, rather than a *fatwa* as such) on February 14, 1989, that the author of the book and its publishers were "sentenced to death." It would appear that Khomeini initially dismissed the book and its author as insignificant, but came to believe (or to be persuaded) after demonstrations against it in Kashmir, Pakistan, and the United Kingdom, that action against it could be politically useful—rather as he had made the hostage crisis politically useful in 1979–1981. In the West, the hokm was widely (though not universally) condemned as an unacceptable attack on free speech, and served to deepen the distaste with which the Iranian regime was generally regarded, thus deepening further Iran's international isolation.

The book's central themes were largely about cultural exile and were not blasphemous or hostile to Islam, but it included a dream sequence in which prostitutes took the names of the Prophet Mohammad's wives, and explored a much older apocryphal story that the devil had attempted to insert subversive verses into the Qoran. Many Muslims were offended by what they were told about it.

Khomeini's declaration against the book and against Rushdie came at a time when Khomeini and those around him were realizing that his death was not far off, and that it would present new challenges for the Islamic Republic. Khomeini wanted above all to secure the continuation of the Islamic Republic in the form that he had created for it. The anti-western, antiliberal aspect of the Islamic Republic was, for him and others, an expression of its religious core and of Iran's independence. The deepening of Iran's international isolation was not, for Khomeini, an unfortunate side effect of the hokm; it was a part of its central purpose. In addition, after the conclusion of the Iran-Iraq war, which he had felt personally as a failure and a humiliation, the Rushdie affair was an opportunity to reassert Iran's claim to be leading the Islamic world.

The specific juncture at which Khomeini's order against Rushdie came was also significant. February 11, 1989, was the tenth anniversary of the revolution, and around that occasion some senior figures in Iran had criticized the regime's conduct of affairs since 1979, particularly about the war. Montazeri had been specially outspoken, saying, "The people of the world thought our only task here in Iran was to kill." In that context, Khomeini's action over Rushdie appears characteristic of him. It answered criticism not with compromise, but with a radical, intransigent, and unexpected stroke, transcending the criticism by going to an even greater extreme than the conduct previously criticized. The hokm against Rushdie demanded a renewal of commitment from the regime's adherents, undercut wishy-washy liberal sympathizers, and made restoration of normal relations with western countries much more difficult for the best part of a decade thereafter. Finally, in 1998, the British and Iranian governments agreed a set of joint statements in which the Iranians committed themselves not to take any action to threaten Rushdie's life nor to encourage or assist anyone else to do so. This effectively ended the affair as an intergovernmental dispute, though some groups since then have reaffirmed their commitment to the so-called fatwa.

In the meantime Rushdie himself went into hiding, his Japanese translator was murdered, his Norwegian and Italian translators were seriously injured in attacks, and in Turkey in 1993 his Turkish translator narrowly escaped a fire set by a mob that killed thirty-five or more people.

How did the Islamic Republic change after Khomeini's death in 1989?

The Rushdie affair, from an Iranian perspective, was part of a series of developments within Iran that, along with Khomeini's death, changed the Islamic Republic in a series of important ways. But in a sense, they changed things in order that they could stay the same. Khomeini was remarkably successful in ensuring that, in essentials, the Islamic Republic would stay on the course he had set for long after his death.

Through the mid-1980s there had been a series of confrontations between left and right factions within the

Islamic Revolutionary Party (IRP). For the most part, the left faction had been strong in the Majles, while the right faction had controlled the Guardian Council, which had responsibility for vetting legislation for acceptability according to Islam before it could be passed into law. Repeatedly measures on land reform or for the nationalization of foreign trade, for example, were agreed by the Majles only to be rejected by the Guardian Council, producing a stalemate. Behind this lay the enthusiasm of left-leaning politicians for wealth redistribution and the improvement of living conditions for the poorest in society on the one hand (underpinned by the conviction that the drive for greater social justice had been one of the essential purposes of the revolution), and conservative-minded clerics backed by bazaari connections on the other, who were concerned to protect traditional privileges and property rights, in accordance with Islamic law. In fact, the question of how to run an economy according to Islamic principles, much discussed in 1979–1981, was never really resolved; the effect of the war was merely to adjourn the question.

Wartime conditions favored the statist, interventionist economic policies of the left, but Khomeini was careful to keep left and right in balance, backing now one side and now the other. His nominated successor, Montazeri, favored the left. The prime minister for most of the mid-1980s was Mir-Hosein Mousavi, who proved skillful, with his other ministers, in managing the fiscal policy that brought Iran through the war; he also was on the left. The president, however, Ali Khamenei, was aligned with the right and had close connections with the Guardian Council. Rafsanjani was Speaker of the Majles and avoided being overidentified with any faction, but he was thought of as being closer to the right than the left.

Frustrated by factionalism within the IRP, Khomeini abolished it in June 1987, but that move did little to resolve the problem. Around the end of that year he intervened in what appeared initially to be a relatively minor matter over the administration of public utilities, to make a statement in favor of the powers of the state. Khamenei made an unwise attempt to spin this with a statement explaining what Khomeini had really meant to say, and he was rewarded with one of Khomeini's characteristic blasts, asserting a new doctrine of Absolute Guardianship (*velayat-e motlaq*), effectively saying that the interests of the Islamic state trumped any other consideration—including the normal terms of shari'a law and duties of Muslims like prayer, fasting, and the *hajj* pilgrimage. This was a major change, further subordinating traditional Shi'a values and expectations to the brutal necessities of politics, and potentially putting enormous power in the hands of the leading politicians in the state. The left were jubilant, but their celebration was short-lived. In February 1988 a new body was established, the Expediency Council (Majma-e Tashkis-e Maslahat-e Nezam), with the responsibility of arbitrating between the Majles and the Guardian Council. Then, in April 1989, with Khomeini manifestly ailing, the Assembly of Experts was convened to make further constitutional changes. These included the abolition of the office of prime minister, and an amendment to permit the appointment of someone who was not a *marja* to be Supreme Leader.

This had become necessary because Montazeri had finally, definitively fallen from grace. In the summer of 1988 one of Saddam's final attacks had included a push by the Mojahedin-e Khalq Organisation (MKO) forces he had equipped with tanks and other weapons toward Kermanshah. They were destroyed by Iranian forces, but there had been talk of a rising within Iran by MKO sympathizers in support of the offensive. In response, Khomeini ordered the execution in prison of all MKO members who would not recant their beliefs. It is hard to avoid the inference that this terrible decision reflected his bitterness at having to accept the cease-fire ending the war. It is possible also that, like the Rushdie affair later, Khomeini meant to use the killings as a test of loyalty and revolutionary commitment. The killings went on through the late summer and early autumn of 1988, drawing in Tudeh members and other political prisoners also. There is no precise, reliable figure for the numbers killed but it was probably at least four thousand to five thousand. It remains the most shameful episode in the history of the Islamic Republic. Even today some Iranians are reluctant to believe that Khomeini ordered it, but the evidence is clear.

Montazeri protested the killings, and later on his protests became public in Iran when they were broadcast by the BBC in March 1989. For Khomeini this was a personal betrayal, and he finally decided at this point that Montazeri had to be replaced. But there was no obvious replacement. Clerical candidates with the necessary religious credentials were either not reliable or not politically savvy. Those that were reliable did not have the religious credentials. Once again necessity, expediency (*maslahat*), the interests of the state, won the argument. The chosen successor was Ali Khamenei. Khamenei was not a *marja*, not even an ayatollah, so the solution was to change the constitution.

On the day of Khomeini's funeral, June 6, 1989, millions of Iranians flocked to the burial site, and there were chaotic scenes as Sepah troops tried to control them and protect the coffin. By then, Iran already had a new leader. Ali Khamenei had been acclaimed as such on June 4, within hours of Khomeini's death on June 3. It was all very smoothly managed; Rafsanjani was the key figure orchestrating the process. The fact that the new constitutional arrangements were not yet technically in force seemed not to trouble anyone; the Assembly of Experts finished their deliberations on July 8 and a referendum ratified their decisions at the end of the month (July 28). Rafsanjani was elected president in an election held at the same time.

Khomeini's personal charisma and popularity played a large part in the revolution of 1979, and are important in explaining why the regime established by the Iranian revolution was relatively stable, by comparison with what happened after the French revolution, for example. But Khomeini's unique role created problems for the constitution, because his death left such a big hole—this latent problem was known from the beginning, from when the constitution was drafted in 1979. Would liberal tendencies and the influence of the West reassert themselves after his death? Would factionalism destroy the stability of the Islamic republic? The removal of Montazeri, the changes to the constitution, the establishment of the Khamenei-Rafsanjani duumvirate, even the Rushdie affair, were all, it seems, measures Khomeini took in his last months to avoid those dangers. Many rulers have tried, and failed, to influence posthumous events in this way; by comparison with most of them, Khomeini was remarkably successful. But it is worth noting that Rafsanjani was important in managing many of the changes, and his memoirs are also among the most important sources for our knowledge about the way they were arrived at. It is possible that some of the decisions at least (notably, the selection of Khamenei as Khomeini's successor) reflected Rafsanjani's influence rather than originating with Khomeini himself. New source material may someday shed more light on these matters.

What went wrong for Rafsanjani as president in 1989–1997?

No Iranian president has been as powerful as Rafsanjani was after his election in July 1989. Before the constitutional changes that were made that year, the office of president, caught between Khomeini as leader and the prime minister who actually ran the government, was rather squeezed out of relevance. With the office of prime minister abolished and its responsibilities rolled into that of the president, Rafsanjani's role was much more significant. In addition, Khamenei, in the early days of his time as leader, looked unsure of himself; his limited religious credentials just emphasized the contrast with his larger-than-life predecessor. Again, this gave Rafsanjani more room to assert himself.

From the start, the dominant theme of Rafsajani's presidency was reconstruction. The eight-year war with Iraq had left the country a mess. Massive investment was needed in the war zone, and in cities away from the front that had been hit by long-range rocket attacks and bombing, to replace and repair destroyed and damaged infrastructure and housing. It has been estimated that the war itself, by the end, had cost Iran around 200 billion dollars, and that GDP had fallen by 1988 to 54 percent of its peak level in 1976. There were large numbers of refugees in the country from Afghanistan and, after 1991, from Iraq—more than two million in total by the mid-1990s. The UN estimated that there were sixteen million mines scattered over the war zone in Iranian territory—clearing them was a laborious, slow, and dangerous business (and still incomplete in the second decade of the twenty-first century). Large numbers of skilled people from a range of economic sectors had left Iran. Much capital had fled the country also—the *Tehran Times* estimated around 120 billion dollars.

Price controls and subsidies for consumer staples during the war had the effect of further weakening the nonoil sector in Iran's quasi-rentier economy. The import of raw materials had been difficult, and the demands of war had diverted investment away from productive industry. Many factories, Rafsanjani admitted in the summer of 1989, were operating at only 20, 30, or 40 percent of their potential capacity. The economy was heavily dependent on oil (90 percent of foreign exchange receipts), and nearly a third of those in employment had jobs in the public sector. Consumer price inflation is believed to have risen from 18.9 percent in 1986 to 24 percent in 1987 and 25.4 percent in 1988. The government had encouraged a high birth rate during the war—it had risen from levels that were already high prewar to give a rate of annual population growth of 3.9 percent in 1986: among the highest in the world at the time. Iran's population went from thirty-eight million in 1979 to sixty million in 1990 (estimated around eighty million in 2015). More than half the population were under twenty years of age in the early 1990s and nearly a third were under ten years old. This contributed to high unemployment; the official figure was 14 percent, but private estimates suggested around 26 percent and youth unemployment was even higher.

From early on Rafsanjani recognized that the question of how to repair the economy was going to reopen deep-seated political differences about economic policy that had been left unresolved since the revolution. Unlike Iraq, which had financed the latter part of its war effort by running heavily into debt, Iran had largely avoided debt by 1988. But Rafsanjani soon began to borrow heavily in order to pay for investment after mid-1989, despite some adverse comment from political opponents.

Rafsanjani's economic policy enjoyed some early success, achieving growth rates of 12.1 percent in 1990–1991 and 9.9 percent in 1991–1992. Nonoil exports rose and so did agricultural production. But then things began to go wrong. Having risen at the time of Saddam's invasion of Kuwait in August 1990, the oil price fell again, from thirty dollars a barrel to around fourteen dollars. With import levels high and revenue falling, foreign debt ballooned (to an estimated thirty billion dollars) and the government had to devote a large part of foreign exchange revenue to the servicing of its debts. The national currency fell on the foreign exchanges against the dollar, and an official devaluation in late 1993 failed to halt a further slide. Devaluation made imports and the servicing of foreign debt more expensive and further boosted domestic inflation, which reached 35 percent in 1993—and perhaps as high as 50 percent.

Rafsanjani's economic difficulties hit his reputation hard. He had presented himself as a fixer, a pragmatist, with the practical skills to put right the country's ills— skills that (by implication) his clerical colleagues and more ideological revolutionary peers mostly lacked. The currency crisis was especially damaging—few things humiliate a government in peacetime more than a currency devaluation, because the currency is a symbol of nationhood itself and its economic strength. He was reelected as president in 1993, but with a reduced turnout, and in his second term he faced more opposition from a more rightwing Majles. He made some progress toward privatization, but then the Majles intervened to ensure that privatized businesses were mostly taken over by *Bonyad* (charitable foundations)—which effectively meant continuation of state control in another form. His efforts to reduce Iran's isolation and secure foreign investment were stymied by Iran's continuing terrorist connections, by the unresolved Rushdie affair, and by the Iran-Libya Sanctions Act passed in the United States in 1996.

By the end of Rafsanjani's time as president in 1997, there was widespread disillusionment, not just with him (his reputation was further tainted by rumors of corruption in his family) but with the whole ruling clique of the Islamic Republic. Living standards for the poorest were still low and had not greatly improved. Unemployment was high. There were complaints that projects to repair war damage had still not been realized. In addition, people chafed at restrictions on press freedom and political activity, and the casual arrogance of some close to the *nezam* (the system) who behaved as if the state belonged to them and always would.

Why did attempts at reform fail under Khatami, during 1997–2005?

The discontents that had grown through the period of Rafsanjani's presidency came together in the unexpected election of Mohammad Khatami as president in May 1997. Khatami had served as the Minister for Islamic Guidance under Mir-Hosein Mousavi, and again briefly under Rafsanjani, but had been forced to resign by hard-liners indignant at his tentative efforts to expand freedom of speech. In the presidential elections of 1997, Khatami was an outsider, but he won partly because the approved regime candidate was incompetent and partly because he had the help of people in the media he had met through his ministerial job previously. But he also won because his advocacy of reform, greater freedom of speech, and what he called civil society captured the imagination of many Iranians, especially women, ethnic minorities, students, and the young generally. His personal modesty, quiet charm, and intellectual earnestness also won him votes. As polling day grew closer, enthusiasm for Khatami's candidacy grew; in the end there was an 80 percent turnout and Khatami got 70 percent of the vote—an overwhelming success.

The reform movement was broader than just Khatami. A number of other former leftist politicians, like him, had moved to a more liberal position, advocating more political freedom. Ayatollah Montazeri, Khomeini's sometime successor, now bitterly opposed to Khamenei and under house arrest, gave Khatami his support. Several religious intellectuals (Kadivar, Soroush, Shabestari, Eshkevari) were arguing for a more liberal version of the Islamic Republic, congruent with Khatami's vision.

In the first three years of his presidency, Khatami's electoral success was sustained by a huge expansion in press activity. Large numbers of new newspapers and journals appeared, most of them with a pro-reform editorial position. His efforts to open up Iranian foreign policy and improve relations with the West also had some success; his government negotiated a successful resolution of the Rushdie affair, permitting an enhancement of diplomatic relations with the United Kingdom and other EU countries, and in an interview with CNN in the autumn of 1997 he even hinted that there could be some improvement in relations with the United States.

But the hard-line right in the circle around Khamenei, in the Guardian Council, the Iranian Ministry of Information and Security (MOIS—the Iranian secret police), and the Revolutionary Guard had no sympathy for Khatami or his reform program, and worked almost from the start to destabilize his government. And Khatami's government never made much headway with economic reform that might have benefited the large numbers of underprivileged people who had voted for him hoping for better in 1997.

Rather than strike at Khatami directly, the hard-liners at first attacked his ministers. Two were prosecuted and imprisoned, and a third was forced out of office. A series of killings of writers, journalists, and liberal-oriented politicians at the end of 1998 culminated early in 1999 with a shocking admission from the MOIS that a so-called rogue element from within that organization had been responsible. The murders were widely interpreted as another attempt to weaken Khatami's government; Khatami achieved a success in forcing the MOIS to take responsibility. In May 2000 the reformists achieved a further success in the Majles elections, securing a majority of delegates. Some thought this would mean that the reformists would finally be enabled to motor ahead with their reform program, with a democratic mandate, but they were disappointed.

In the last months of the previous Majles, a new, more restrictive press law had been passed. The new Majles intended from the start to overturn the press law as a matter of priority, but when they moved to do so Khamenei intervened personally, with a letter forbidding it. Over the summer of 2000 many of the reformist papers were closed down. Some journalists persevered, opening new newspapers under different titles, but they were closed too, and some journalists and editors were arrested and imprisoned. The space for free speech that had opened up in the first three years of Khatami's presidency was gradually shut down, though not without a struggle. The press freedom question was emblematic for Khatami's project as a whole. From the summer of 2000 his presidency was effectively crippled (despite his being reelected for a second term in 2001). Further attempts to bring forward reforming legislation went through the Majles but were rejected by the Guardian Council and prevented from becoming law.

Nonetheless, Khatami's attempt at reform of the Islamic Republic was not a total failure. It inspired and motivated a generation of young people, encouraging them to persist with their aspirations. Many journalists and others in the country continued to regard themselves as reformists and continued to push for their beliefs when any opportunity offered itself. Women continued to push against the limits of the dress code that had shifted in a more relaxed direction during Khatami's time—a highly visible and significant form of protest. A few years later the reformist cause resurfaced in the Green Movement (see the account of the 2009 presidential election in chapter 6).

How has the Islamic regime treated minorities since the revolution?

As in other matters, the impression one gets of Iran's ethnic and religious composition from outside is misleading. The standard impression of the Islamic Republic is of a fairly homogeneous population of Persian-speaking Shi'a Muslims, but the reality is much more diverse.

If one takes a maximalist view of minorities in Iran, including, for example, Iranians from the Caspian coast region speaking Mazanderani and Gilaki dialects as minorities rather than as part of the dominant Persian-speaking group, then that Persian-speaking group could itself (narrowly) be a minority overall. But if one counts them as part of the main group of Shi'a Persian speakers, then that group accounts for about 60 percent of the total population, and ethnic and religious minorities make up 40 percent of the total. Within that 40 percent, Azeri Turks are by far the largest minority, with 16 percent of the total population. Next come the Kurds (10 percent of the total), then the Lurs (6 percent—including Bakhtiari), Arabs, Baluch (2 percent or less each), Talysh, Qashqai, and Turkmen (about 1 percent each) and then the remainder (Armenians, Georgians, Assyrian Christians, Jews), making up another 1 percent among them. In religious terms, Iran is more homogeneous; 90 percent of the population are Twelver Shi'a Muslims, 8 percent are Sunni (mainly Baluchis, Turkmen, Kurds, and some Arabs), and about 2 percent belong to other religious groups (Christians, Jews, Zoroastrians, Yazidis, Mandaeans, etc.). Bahais may be as numerous as the Christians (perhaps 300,000 to 350,000), but the circumstances of their persecution make it difficult to estimate their numbers accurately and they do not appear in official figures because the Islamic Republic does not acknowledge the Bahai faith as such.

Of all the minorities, the Azeris are the most assimilated. As explained earlier in this book, rulers and dynasties of Turkic origin have played a major part in Iranian history. Many prominent clerics and politicians in contemporary Iran come from an Azeri background, including Ali Khamenei himself, and Mir-Hosein Mousavi (who are themselves related). There is some support for Azeri separatist groups, but it is not a major issue in national or local politics, despite attempts since 1989 by some within the newly independent state of Azerbaijan to the north to excite pan-Turkish and separatist sentiments.

Of the remainder, the Kurds are the minority group that has been most consistent in calling for more autonomy (at least), followed by the Baluchis and the Arabs. All these groups (including some of the more outspoken Azeris) complain that their minority status has meant economic and developmental deprivation under the Islamic Republic. Levels of educational attainment are distinctly lower among these groups; Kurds and Baluchis attribute this to the poorer standard of teaching that results from their children having to learn in a second language because the central government insists that teaching be conducted in Persian. They also say that they are always at the back of the queue when it comes to central funding for development projects (in addition, the Kurdestan region was affected disproportionally by the damaging effects of the Iran-Iraq war). There has been an element of Persian chauvinism in the way that these and other minorities have been treated by the central government, as well as an element of more or less paranoid nationalism: minorities calling for greater autonomy have routinely been accused of colluding with foreign powers.

The three main non-Muslim religious minorities, Christians, Jews, and Zoroastrians, have a unique privilege in that they are represented in the Majles by their own representatives, who are appointed independently from the procedures used to elect other deputies. This reflects the clear position in shari'a law that adherents of these religions, as "People of the Book," should be tolerated and respected within Muslim society. Nonetheless, relations between these communities and the Islamic Republic have been uneasy at best, and there have been episodes of active persecution. For the Christians, tension has tended to revolve around suspicion that Christians are proselytizing to convert Muslims to Christianity—evangelical protestant sects are more suspect than the traditional Armenian and Assyrian Christians. Jews are suspect because of possible connections to Israel; many Iranian Jews have emigrated to Israel since the 1940s, and especially since 1979—though more have probably emigrated to the United States. Estimates for the number of Jews remaining in the country range from around 20,000 to 30,000—still the largest group anywhere in the Middle East outside Israel. Jews are obliged publicly to subscribe to anti-Zionist political positions, and have sometimes been pressured to donate money to anti-Zionist causes. In 1999 a group of Jews from Shiraz were arrested on charges of spying for Israel; it was widely assumed that their arrest was part of the continuing duel between President Khatami and his hard-line opponents. They were all eventually released, but the episode showed habits of thought in the MOIS. For most members of these minorities the key to a tolerable life that avoids trouble is keeping a low profile and avoiding the attention of the authorities.

Bahais have been treated worse than any other minority group in the Islamic Republic—this is mainly because they are regarded as apostates from Islam, but also because

some believe their faith was favored by the British, and/
or by the Shah in the past, or that it is secretly allied in
the present with Israel. In August 1980 the regime arrested
all nine members of the Bahai National Spiritual Assembly
of Iran. None of them were ever seen again. The Bahais
elected another nine to the assembly—all but one of those
were arrested and secretly executed. Killings continued,
until (according to the Bahais) 177 had been killed by the
end of 1984. Persecution has continued since then at a less
intense pitch, but still with occasional killings and disap-
pearances. In the late 1990s young Bahais were prevented
from attending university; when they set up their own
study groups some of those involved were arrested for alleged conspiracy, and there were more deaths.

In formal terms, the protection afforded to minorities by
the constitution and by Islamic law should protect members of all these groups. But as in other ways, there is a gap
between theory and practice in the Islamic Republic. It is
no excuse to say that many other states in the Middle East
have a record as bad, or worse.

Have social problems like unemployment and drug addiction got better or worse since 1989?

The revolution of 1979 was not just a political revolution or
a coup—it was a genuine social revolution that eclipsed the
privilege of previously powerful classes and gave opportunities to many that had previously little hope of advance-
ment. Part of the rhetoric, and to some extent the reality
of the revolution (especially for those on the left), was that
it was for the *mostazafin*—the oppressed—that they somehow owned the revolution and should be its prime ben-
eficiaries. But as in other times and places, the grip of the
privileged on their privileges was hard to shake, and the
hardships of the mostazafin as a class have proved hard to

eradicate, however successful a few have been in escaping their deprived origins.

The main reason for obstinately high levels of poverty in Iran has been the high level of unemployment. Since 2000 official figures show unemployment fluctuating between 10 percent and 14 percent, with youth unemployment (young people between the ages of fifteen and twenty-nine) roughly double that—between 22 percent and 29 percent, and for young women around 40 percent. But many economists have serious doubts about the accuracy of Iranian official statistics; some have suggested that the real overall figure is nearer 20 percent, with youth unemployment nearer 40 percent and even a figure of 85 percent for young people under the age of twenty-five.

High unemployment is a sign of underlying weaknesses in the Iranian economy. The economy simply has not grown at the rates necessary to supply new jobs for the large numbers of young people coming onto the labor market each year (the birth rate moderated in the 2000s after the exuberant levels of the 1980s and 1990s, but more than 60 percent of Iran's roughly eighty million people were under thirty years old in 2015). In the early 1990s it was possible to blame the effects of the Iran-Iraq war for Iran's poor economic performance; more recently the regime has blamed sanctions (especially after much tougher sanctions were applied after November 2011). But the Iranian economy has long languished under a number of structural problems that have been independent of other factors. Excessive dependence on oil is the central underlying problem; even though Iran is not so heavily dependent on oil as some oil-rich states in the Middle East region, it does display many of the depressing features of what are classified as rentier economies, in which income from one state-controlled source stultifies and smothers other areas of economic activity. One feature of rentier states is the tendency toward an overdeveloped public sector—a factor exaggerated further in Iran by the statist tendency that inevitably took effect during the period of the Iran-Iraq war—producing a significant degree of what could be called concealed unemployment in addition to the overt kind. Other observers have noted the way that rentierism tends to shore up authoritarian states and to impede the development and political influence of an independent middle class. These are phenomena that one can also see at work in Iran.

High unemployment brings with it a familiar train of other social problems—one of the most serious being drug addiction. Iran lies squarely on the drug-trafficking highway for opium and heroin from Afghanistan to Europe. There are large numbers of Afghan refugees in Iran who are readily visible in the poorer parts of many Iranian cities, and some of them are involved in the drug trade. The UN World Drug Report suggested in 2010 that 20 percent of Iranians between the ages of fifteen and sixty were involved in illegal drug use—this being one of the highest levels of drug abuse in the world. Drug addiction entails further damaging social problems, including various criminal activities, and is related to the levels of prostitution.

Under the Islamic Republic, unemployment has repercussions one would not expect in other countries. Young people without jobs cannot set up independent households or get married—up to 75 percent of Iranians in their twenties still live with their parents. They cannot legally have sexual relations—yet in fact some commentators have pointed to the springing up of a huge new underground sex culture among young people. Those that do marry have increasingly often got divorced—the proportion of marriages ending in divorce rose from 12 percent to 21 percent between 2007 and 2014—a development that may have had something to do with changing expectations, especially among women, but also with economic stress, levels of addiction, and so on. The combination of these different phenomena—unemployment, poverty, addiction, marital breakdown, prostitution, all of which affect young people disproportionately—has led some to suggest that Iran is undergoing a kind of social breakdown. The World Happiness Report compiled for 2015 by the Earth Institute at Columbia University placed Iran at 110 in a list of 158 countries.

Does Iran support terrorism?

Prime among the US government's reasons for bringing in the Iran-Libya Sanctions Act in 1996 (though there were also concerns about human rights and the nuclear question) were concerns over the Iranian government's support for groups like Lebanese Hezbollah, Islamic Jihad, and Hamas who were committed to the destruction of Israel, including through the use of violence and terrorist methods. Many of the violent incidents that have been connected with the Islamic Republic have also involved Islamic Jihad and/or Lebanese Hezbollah and have been directed at Israel. Others, more directly associated with the regime, have been aimed at political figures regarded as enemies of the state.

Islamic Jihad were responsible for two huge suicide bombings in Beirut in April and October 1983, wrecking the US embassy and two barracks near the airport, respectively. Sixty-three died at the embassy and nearly three hundred at the barracks, which had been occupied by US Marines and French paratroopers that had been serving in Lebanon as peacekeeping troops. The incidents followed a series of developments in which, after the foreign troops had been welcomed initially, feeling turned against them when US warships fired on positions inland in support of the Lebanese army. After the barracks bombings, the US and other international peacekeeping troops pulled out of Lebanon. In November, the Israeli military headquarters in Tyre was hit by a suicide bomb, killing twenty-eight Israelis. The Israelis hit the Iranian base in the Bekaa in retaliation, killing twenty-three Sepah.

In July 1989 Abdul Rahman Qasemlu, head of the Kurdestan Democratic Party of Iran (KDPI), was murdered in Vienna in the middle of negotiations with representatives of the Iranian government (in fact, they were members of the MOIS). Two of the alleged perpetrators were released by the Austrian government, after the Iranian government threatened reprisals if they were prosecuted. In August 1991 Shapur Bakhtiar (who had been prime minister briefly at the beginning of 1979 as the Shah left Iran) was assassinated at his home in Paris. He had been active in exile politics against the Islamic regime and had survived an earlier attempt on his life in July 1980. One of the perpetrators was arrested and convicted; when he was later released (in 2010) he returned to Tehran.

In March 1992 a suicide bomb in a truck destroyed the Israeli embassy in Buenos Aires, Argentina, along with a number of other nearby buildings (including a school). Nearly thirty people were killed, and hundreds were injured, most of them Argentine citizens with no connection to the embassy, some of them children. Islamic Jihad claimed responsibility, saying that the bombing was retribution for Israel's killing of a Lebanese Hezbollah chief; but the United States claimed they had evidence of Iranian state involvement also. In July 1994 a second vehicle-based suicide bomb destroyed the Asociación Mutual Israelita Argentina (a Jewish community center) in Buenos Aires, killing eighty-five and injuring more than two hundred. This time there was no claim of responsibility. Investigators later came to believe that a member of Lebanese Hezbollah had been the perpetrator, and have alleged that Mohsen

Rabbani, a cleric serving at the time as a cultural attaché at the Iranian embassy in Buenos Aires, had facilitated both attacks. But the local investigation of the latter bombing in particular has been inconclusive and unsatisfactory, and has become a high-level scandal in Argentine politics in its own right.

In September 1992 three Iranian Kurdish leaders, including Sadegh Sharafkandi, were murdered with their translator at the Mykonos restaurant in Berlin. Sharafkandi had been Abdul Rahman Qasemlu's successor as head of the KDPI after Qasemlu's assassination in Vienna. An Iranian and a Lebanese were arrested and eventually convicted for the killings—when the convictions came through (in April 1997) the Berlin judge issued international arrest warrants for the Iranian intelligence minister, Ali Fallahian, as well as for Rafsanjani and Khamenei.

The United States have blamed Iran for involvement in the Khobar Towers bombing of June 1996 in Saudi Arabia (which killed nineteen US servicemen and one Saudi, and injured 372). In 2001 the FBI issued an indictment, based partly on classified information, and in 2015 a Saudi Shi'a named in the indictment was arrested in Beirut. But on other occasions the Saudi government seemed to be blaming Al Qaeda for the attack—a connection with an Al Qaeda car bombing in Riyadh the previous November has been suggested—and there have been indications that Osama bin Laden himself claimed responsibility. In addition, much of the evidence behind the FBI indictment appears to have been based on confessions of dubious validity, extracted by the Saudi authorities under torture.

Those are the main terrorist incidents or assassinations that have been linked to Iran. Since the mid-1990s the accusation that Iran still supports terrorism has been based largely on Iran's backing for Hamas and Lebanese Hezbollah, and the connection with their violent acts toward Israel, but the rogue state impression has been supported by Islamic Jihad's previous hostage-taking activities in Lebanon, the Rushdie affair, and (later, after 2000) the growing disquiet over Iran's nuclear program. Nonetheless, those inclined to notice have seen that since the terrorist attacks on the United States on 9/11 in particular, Iran has had little or no direct involvement in terrorism (and a consensus has emerged among Shi'a clerics that suicide attacks, in particular, are unacceptable in principle). Meanwhile Sunni Muslim terrorism, drawing on the growing global influence of Saudi-supported Wahhabism, whether under the flag of Al Qaeda or Islamic State/Daesh or others, using suicide bombing or other tactics, has burgeoned hugely (and has often, especially in Iraq and Pakistan, been directed at Shi'a Muslims). There were reports in the summer of 2015, following the nuclear settlement between Iran and the P5 + 1, that Iran had ceased funding support for Hamas. One can only hope that the downward trend in Iran's involvement in terrorism, observable since the latter part of the presidency of Hashemi Rafsanjani, will be sustained.

What is so special about Iranian cinema?

In 1978 and 1979 cinemas, along with police stations, SAVAK offices, and banks—all regarded as symbols either of state repression or of foreign interference—were often targeted by revolutionary crowds who broke windows and ransacked the premises. The burning of the Rex Cinema in Abadan in August 1978, in which several hundred people lost their lives, was part of that phenomenon (see chapter 4) and was a significant moment in the rising crescendo of the revolution. Islamic revolutionaries regarded film and cinema primarily as vehicles for immorality and alien western values.

Accordingly, immediately after the revolution, the screening of foreign films and the making of Iranian films alike became almost impossible. But within a few years, under the pressure of war, the regime realized the potential propaganda value of film. Restrictions were relaxed to a certain extent, and some funding was made available to filmmakers (from 1982). Iranian filmmakers benefited from restrictions that meant only a few western films were shown in Iranian cinemas each year—competition was largely removed. As we have seen, literary figures in Iran have in the past had an almost heroic status, and under the Pahlavis literature had been a medium for the dissemination of political ideas and political dissent. Under the Islamic Republic, for the most part, censorship put an end to this phenomenon (with some exceptions, notably the poet Ahmad Shamlu). Censorship tended to gag or stultify literary efforts, making independent-minded writers and poets reluctant to risk committing their real thoughts to paper. But although literature in Iran since the revolution has languished, cinema somehow flourished despite the constraints and in some sense took its place in cultural leadership. The restrictions of censorship, rather than crippling creativity completely, seem rather to have made Iranian film more subtle, delivering artistic and often social and political messages all the more effectively for being allusive and indirect.

Prevented by censorship from following the tendency in Hollywood to exploit sex and violence to manipulate audiences, and avoiding the related tendency toward ever-faster cutting and editing of scenes, Iranian films took a different path. They avoided trouble by a variety of strategies. Some did so by taking children as their protagonists (like in *Where Is the Friend's Home* in 1987; *Bashu, the Little Stranger* in 1990; or *The White Balloon* in 1995). Many were made in a quasi-documentary, fly-on-the-wall style. Restrictions were relaxed further, for a time, under Khatami's presidency, and films produced by or about Iran's ethnic minorities appeared, notably Bahman Ghobadi's *A Time for Drunken Horses* and *Turtles Can Fly*, set in Iranian and Iraqi Kurdestan, respectively. There has been a divide in Iranian cinema between sometimes inaccessible high-art films like Mohsen Makhmalbaf's *Kandahar* or Abbas Kiarostami's *Taste of Cherry*, which won prizes at western film festivals but had less appeal for mass audiences, and the thrillers and romantic comedies that Iranian cinemas show in their standard programs (which seldom get seen outside Iran). War films, drawing on the experience of the Iran-Iraq war, have also been a plentiful and popular genre.

Other filmmakers have turned popular cinema into something more sophisticated, making political points along the way. One example of this was Kamal Tabrizi's *Marmoulak (The Lizard)* from 2004, which initially managed to evade the censors despite satirizing the clergy, before eventually being banned after drawing large audiences who cheered and clapped in the theaters. Another (very different) film that was successful both as entertainment and artistically (and which did well outside Iran also) was Asghar Farhadi's *A Separation* (2011). But perhaps the most successful director to deliver plot-driven films that are also moving and hard-hitting has been Jafar Panahi, with films like *The Circle*, *Crimson Gold*, and *Offside*. Panahi was imprisoned after the mass demonstrations of 2009 and is still under house arrest.

Iranian cinema has served to remind foreigners that the media image of Iran as bleak, harsh, and politically repressed is not the whole story, and with its poetic intensity and moral commitment has reasserted the link back to the cultural achievements of Iran's great poets, philosophers, artists, and architects in earlier centuries.

6

AHMADINEJAD, ROUHANI AND IRAN NOW

How did Ahmadinejad become president in 2005?

Among the presidents Iran has had since the revolution, Mahmoud Ahmadinejad was the joker in the pack. He was not part of the charmed circle of regime insiders who had held positions of power and influence since 1979. Unlike many of them, he came not from a clerical or middle-class background but from lower-class or lower-middle-class origins, and attended a vocational higher education institution rather than an elite one. He had a doctorate in road-traffic management (having studied for it part-time over a period of years). His usual clothing was downbeat and unfashionable to the point of antifashionable. Other Iranians, including politicians, from more privileged backgrounds, joked and jeered at his supposed ignorance and lack of refinement. But he showed no shame about any of this—rather he took pride in it and turned it all to his advantage. Rather than attempt to appeal to the educated middle classes and those who aspired to that status, he appealed instead to the less educated, the poor and ordinary people who were suspicious or resentful of the reformists and the ruling elite in general. Both within Iran and in Iran's external relations, his trademark was *por-rui* (cheekiness), and an insolent disregard for the conventional norms of politics.

Ahmadinejad first came to the attention of the Iranian public when he was elected mayor of Tehran in 2003. As mayor, he made the news with would-be populist right-wing gestures and made much of his Sepah connections, giving large construction contracts to Sepah contractors, for example. This was a phase in which disillusionment with Khatami's reform project was growing among ordinary Iranians. Some blamed Khatami himself, and his reformist colleagues; the reformists blamed the hard-liners for blocking Khatami's initiatives and the Guardian Council in particular, for vetoing reformist candidates in elections—especially during the 2004 Majles elections. The reformist response—at least the response of some—was to call for a boycott. The turnout in the 2004 Majles elections was low (apparently around 51 percent) as a result, and they produced a strongly right-wing Majles.

The phenomenon was repeated in the 2005 presidential elections. Vetting removed the most credible reformist candidates, and many reformist voters boycotted the election. Turnout in the first round was 62 percent: again low by Iranian standards. Out of seven candidates Hashemi Rafsanjani, bidding for a further presidential term, got the largest number of votes in the first round. The second largest number went to Ahmadinejad, which was a surprise; there had been speculation earlier in the campaign that he might withdraw to give another hard-liner a better chance, but it seems that the leadership circle swung their support behind him in the last few days before the poll. The candidate who came in third (Mehdi Karrubi) called foul and alleged fraud—a claim that was (belatedly) taken more seriously after the more vociferous allegations of fraud in the 2009 elections. The two leading candidates then went through to a second round poll, held a week later. As an ultimate regime insider, living in grand style, rather complacent, Rafsanjani suited Ahmadinejad as an electoral opponent very well. By contrast, Ahmadinejad stressed his humble origins, campaigned vigorously in provincial towns and villages, and emphasized the need to bring oil wealth to the tables of the poorest. On the polling day Rafsanjani tried but failed to bring out reformists in his support, turnout was low again (60 percent), and Ahmadinejad beat him with 60 percent of the poll. Ahmadinejad had come almost from nowhere to take office as president of Iran.

Did Ahmadinejad's provocative statements about the Holocaust reflect a deep-seated Iranian anti-Semitism?

Before Ahmadinejad was elected president, and during his election campaign, he stuck almost exclusively to an internal political agenda, stressing above all the needs of the underprivileged. After he became president he showed a new interest in foreign policy, in the nuclear question, and after a time, in Israel.

He made what became his most notorious statement on Israel as part of a speech in October 2005 (though it was made on a relatively minor occasion and may not have been intended to have the impact it later achieved) when he said "in rejimeh eshghalgareh Qods bayad az safeyeh ruzegar mahv shavad." This was a phrase that had been used years before by Khomeini. Translated literally, it meant "this Jerusalem-occupying regime must disappear from the page of time." But when it was picked up and reported in the West, many used a more succinct translation—"Israel must be wiped from the map." Coupled with the more uncompromising position that Ahmadinejad was taking over the nuclear question at the same time, the statement was taken by some as a straightforward threat to destroy Israel with nuclear weapons.

Ahmadinejad's statement did not depart from the previously established regime position on Israel. Both Rafsanjani and Khamenei had made strong statements in 2001, for example, that had not achieved the coverage outside Iran that Ahmadinejad achieved. But rather than being daunted or dismayed by the reaction he got, Ahmadinejad's response was to go further. In December 2005 he suggested (ignoring significant aspects of the history) that Jews should have been resettled in Germany or Austria after the Holocaust, and asked why the Palestinians should have had to suffer for it. He harped on the same theme several times within a few days, appearing to doubt whether six million Jews had died in the Holocaust, referring to it as a myth, and questioning why this was taboo in the West (and illegal in some countries) when it was possible to insult religion there with impunity. A year later the Iranian Foreign Ministry hosted a bizarre conference of Holocaust deniers in Tehran; in response to the further furor the conference caused internationally, the Foreign Ministry pointed out that there was nothing new in any of this; it had all been said by other Iranian politicians before Ahmadinejad. Nonetheless, other figures within Iran criticized Ahmadinejad and his foreign minister for their conduct over these matters, and for making unnecessary trouble for Iran in its overseas relations. The incident was significant in exposing a gap between Ahmadinejad and other conservatives that grew wider later.

Since the revolution the official position taken by the regime had always been that they were against Israel and against Zionism, but that this did not imply anti-Semitism and that Jews within Iran enjoyed the traditional protection of People of the Book according to the shari'a. During the revolution itself, and particularly on September 8, 1978 (Black Friday), many demonstrators injured with gunshot wounds were taken to the Jewish hospital in Tehran, the Dr. Sapir Hospital, because being privately run it was not under surveillance from SAVAK as most of the other hospitals were, and patients were treated for free. The hospital had a good relationship with Ayatollah Taleqani and its director was given a letter of thanks from Khomeini in Paris. In May 1979 Khomeini met a small delegation of Jewish community leaders in Qom, spoke recognizing the deep roots of Judaism in Iran and the beliefs held in common between Islam and Judaism, and thanked them for their role in the revolution. The meeting was widely reported and was used to establish a clear distinction between the Iranian Jewish community and the Zionism of Israel, and to dispel the idea that Jews were undercover agents for Zionism. Nonetheless, some associated with the regime from time to time let slip loose talk about "the Jews."

Iran's Jewish community can trace its origins all the way back to 720 BC, when the Assyrians conquered the northern kingdom of Israel and Jews resettled to parts of Media. In the Old Testament of the Bible, the Persian kings appear favorably for the most part, as protectors; Cyrus the Great famously allowed Jews to return to Jerusalem from Babylon and rebuild the Temple there. In later centuries a pattern emerged, of lengthy periods of tolerance interspersed with outbreaks of low-level persecution; this was the case under the Safavids and again later under the Qajars. As elsewhere in the Middle East, Jews and Christians were tolerated under religious law (a level of protection that Jews did not enjoy in medieval Europe, for example), but did not have the same rights and privileges as Muslims, and were regarded by some as impure or unclean. If Iranian Jews were in difficulty they often appealed successfully to senior clerics for protection, but lesser or marginal clerics might incite mobs with anti-Semitic rhetoric. There were pogroms against Jews in Tabriz, Hamadan, and Mashhad in the nineteenth century. In the twentieth century European anti-Semitism had an influence within Iran also, lending a spurious scientific authority to preexisting prejudice in some quarters.

As mentioned elsewhere, there is still a large Jewish community in Iran; in other parts of the Middle East such communities have disappeared as Jews have migrated to the United States, Israel, or Europe under the pressure of ill treatment and intolerance. Across the whole of the Middle East today, anti-Semitic language is regrettably common, encouraged by hostility to Israel and sympathy for the Palestinians. But it is probably less common in Iran than elsewhere, despite the current government of the Islamic Republic being more openly hostile to Israel than some others in the region. Many countries, including most European countries, have a history of anti-Semitism. There has been anti-Semitism in Iran too, but it is not a central feature of Iranian culture; there is an ancient tradition of humane tolerance also. The BBC reported a poll in May 2014 that suggested that 56 percent of Iranians held negative views of Jewish people—but this was the lowest figure for any country in the Middle East apart from Israel, compared with 69 percent in Turkey and 93 percent in the Palestinian territories, for example. Despite the offensive posturing of Ahmadinejad and others about the Holocaust, only 18 percent of Iranians believed the statement "Jews still talk too much about what happened to them in the Holocaust" was "probably true"—compared with 22 percent polled in the United States.

Was the Iranian nuclear program intended to produce a nuclear weapon?

The Iranian nuclear program began in the time of Mohammad Reza Shah, with support from Germany and the United States among others. From the beginning there was speculation that it aimed to produce a nuclear weapon, in addition to the overt and declared aim of civil power generation.

Iran has been a signatory of the Nuclear Nonproliferation Treaty (NPT) since its inception in 1968, as a nonnuclear weapon state. Under the Islamic Republic, the nuclear program was initially cancelled in its entirety by Khomeini (who regarded it as one of the Shah's vainglorious extravagances, and considered all weapons of mass destruction to be against Islam). But it was restarted in the mid-1980s when the Iranians became aware that Saddam Hussein was moving forward with a nuclear weapon program. As with other aspects of war policy at that time, and security policy after the end of the war, Rafsanjani appears to have been a major influence in the decision making.

The Iranian regime has repeatedly declared its adherence to the provisions of the NPT, its commitment to solely civil application of nuclear energy, and its religious position that nuclear weapons are against Islam. But uncertainty and suspicion about the intentions of the Iranian nuclear program have persisted in recent years because despite the protestations of the Iranian government, western governments and their intelligence agencies have remained convinced that the Iranian nuclear program has aimed at the creation of a nuclear weapon.

One approach to this would simply be to say, as some have, that the Iranian regime has been lying and that the prime aim of the program must always have been to produce a nuclear weapon. But there is good reason to regard this view as too sweeping. The regime's religious stance against weapons of mass destruction has been consistent since Khomeini's time, and it is, after all, an Islamic Republic. The declared stance takes some added credibility from the fact that Iran could have retaliated against Iraq with chemical weapons in the 1980s, but did not.

It is possible to reconcile the two positions by suggesting that the real intention of the Iranian regime was to acquire the *capability* to produce a nuclear weapon, without actually manufacturing the weapon itself. This would mean that Iran would have the materials and the technical expertise to produce a bomb or warhead within a period of time (perhaps a year or less), if presented with a serious security crisis like an invasion or a destructive bombing campaign. This capability would in itself act as a deterrent to aggression—a lesser degree of deterrent than that provided by a real weapon perhaps, but nonetheless significant and better than nothing. It would also have the advantage of avoiding a breach of Iran's commitments under the NPT, and the dire consequences at the UN that would inevitably follow such a breach. Other countries—notably Japan and Germany—are widely thought to have a similar de facto capability, despite being nonnuclear weapon states under the NPT.

If that is so, then the Iranians never intended to produce an actual weapon, but rather a deterrent capability as an option *in extremis*. Such a position might appear equivocal, but it would not be inconsistent with the terms of international treaty law, and would give Iran a form of deterrence against aggression.

Is Iran a serious threat to Israel?

Iran does not recognize Israel as a legitimate state, and since 1979 has supported groups that deny Israel's right to exist: notably Hamas and Lebanese Hezbollah. Iran has also supported those groups' use of violence against Israel. This is a direct threat to Israel's security from another major regional state, albeit at a relatively low level of intensity (in recent years Hezbollah has confined itself largely to defensive measures against Israeli forces, and there were

reports in the summer of 2015 that Iran had ceased funding to Hamas altogether). Israel has to take it seriously.

The official Iranian position has not greatly changed
since 1979, but the actual relationship between Iran and
Israel has changed a lot in that time. Strange though it
may seem from the perspective of 2016, during the Iran-
Iraq war Israel was probably Iran's most consistent and
reliable supplier of weapons and weapon parts, at a time
when obtaining any weapons was difficult, and increasingly so as the war went on (as explained earlier in the
account of the Iran-Iraq war and Iran/Contra). At the beginning of the war major Israeli politicians like Moshe
Dayan urged the United States to repair relations with Iran
and to support Iran against Iraq. Binyamin Netanyahu
made much more of the threat to Israel from Iran after he
became prime minister in 1996; especially after the fall of
Saddam in 2003 (Israel had previously regarded Iraq as
the more serious threat) and the election of Ahmadinejad
in 2005. As we have seen, Ahmadinejad escalated Iran's
rhetoric against Israel. Netanyahu responded in kind,
claiming that Iran's nuclear program represented an "existential threat."

Significant Israeli figures have criticized Netanyahu for
exaggerating the threat from Iran, implying if not saying
directly that he was partially responsible for escalat-
ing the tension and hostility between the two countries.
These include two retired chiefs of Mossad, and a retired
head of the Israeli internal intelligence service, Shin Bet.
In fact, even if Iran were to acquire a nuclear weapon (already an imaginative leap) it is hard to imagine a scenario
in which Israel's existence could seriously be threatened.
In the modern world, any first use of nuclear weapons
by any state would be the equivalent of putting a knife
to one's own throat. Any use of nuclear weapons by Iran
would be overwhelmed by an annihilating Israeli nuclear

counterstrike, probably augmented by strikes from the United States.

Nonetheless, Iran's denial of Israel's right to exist is serious for Israel. Given the hostility between the two states, Iranian acquisition of any kind of nuclear capability implies a diminution of the effectiveness of Israel's own nuclear deterrent, albeit a small and rather theoretical one. Iran's position on Israel is a relic from the revolution; it takes seriousness from the continuing suffering of the Palestinians, but is a liability in terms of Iran's foreign policy interests. It would benefit Iran and the region as a whole if the Iranian position on Israel could be moderated, at least to a tacit recognition of Israel and a cessation of support for violent acts (as seemed to be implied in the negotiations around the Grand Bargain offer of 2003).

Why did the reelection of Ahmadinejad as president in 2009 cause such a political crisis within Iran?

Stimulated in part by a new phenomenon of televised debates between the candidates, a surge of popular enthusiasm developed in the last few weeks before the presidential elections of June 2009, creating what came to be called the Green Movement. The leading candidate opposing Ahmadinejad's reelection and heading this movement was Mir-Hosein Mousavi, who had served as prime minister during the Iran-Iraq war, but since then had stayed out of politics. Another strand in this mood derived from the election of Barack Obama as president of the United States at the end of the previous year. For those reformist- and moderate-minded Iranians who yearned for an end to Iran's isolation, the policy of the Open Hand toward Iran followed by Obama in the first six months of his presidency, marked in particular by his creative and groundbreaking Nowruz message in March 2009, seemed to offer hope—if only it could be met with a similarly positive response from the Iranian side.

The perception of a growing reform-minded movement behind Mousavi before election day was reinforced by early indications of a high turnout, suggesting that pro-reform voters who had boycotted the elections in 2005 had changed their minds and turned out to vote this time. The votes, when counted, certainly showed a high turnout—85 percent—but they gave Ahmadinejad 63 percent of the vote: well over the 50 percent threshold needed to win the poll outright (less than 50 percent would have meant a second round of voting, with a run-off between the two candidates who had won most votes in the first round).

The reaction was immediate and strong. Tens of thousands of Iranians quickly decided that the election result had been falsified to keep Ahmadinejad in office, and turned out on the streets of Tehran and other cities to protest, wearing scarves or bandanas in green, the color of the Mousavi campaign. Within a few days the number of protestors had grown to hundreds of thousands, with estimates saying a million or more on Monday, June 15. Their numbers and their diverse origins seemed to belie the idea that this was just sour grapes from an isolated group. European and US news media reported excitedly that these were the biggest demonstrations in Iran since the revolution. In the evenings, Iranians gathered on rooftops to shout "Allahu Akbar," as they had in 1978–1979.

No one has proved that the results were falsified, and it may never really be possible to know for sure, but some of the circumstances were suspicious. The results were not presented or announced in the way that previous results had appeared. Against all previous experience in Iranian elections, there was no significant sign of a swing toward candidates in their home districts. Several months before the elections, Supreme Leader Khamenei had made statements supportive of Ahmadinejad that already marked a departure from previous practice. Even before the final results were known, in the small hours of the morning, police and troops were on the streets to forestall demonstrations. They surrounded the Interior Ministry (from which the results were being announced) and Mousavi's campaign headquarters, severely hampering the opposition movement's communications and their ability to respond to events. After the results were announced, Khamenei spoke forcefully in support of Ahmadinejad's reelection within a few hours, acclaiming it as a divine judgment—previously the Supreme Leader had waited until the Guardian Council ratified the result, which usually took three days.

Notwithstanding all this, it is plain that many voters turned out for Ahmadinejad on June 12. The usual judgment is that his support was strongest in conservative rural districts and among the poorer sections of the urban electorate. Voters who distrusted both the regime and the perceived urban sophistication of the opposition candidates, and still were disenchanted with the reformists, voted for Ahmadinejad because unlike other politicians, he looked and sounded like them—they understood him and felt they could trust him. Many Iranians supported his strong stance against the west and in favor of Iran's right to a civil nuclear program. In the countryside it was also easier for the regime to coerce voters—whether by increases in salaries just before the election, or by threats. But one should not go too far (as some have) in characterizing the elections as a confrontation between an urbanized, westernized, vocal minority versus a relatively silent, rural majority. The population of Iran in 2009 was more than 60 percent urban.

Despite beatings and arrests, and despite efforts by the regime to prevent any reporting of the protests, the demonstrations went on, and Iranians found ways to get reporting out of Iran, including through new Internet channels like Facebook and Twitter. Over the summer much of the indignation of the demonstrators was focused on the case of Neda Agha-Soltan, a young woman who had been shot in a demonstration on June 20. Her death was filmed by bystanders using mobile telephones, and was soon seen around the world on YouTube. The demonstrations continued, on and off, for months; often taking advantage of regime-sponsored events and taking them over; for example, on September 18, when the regime attempted to hold its usual event (Qods day—Jerusalem day) to show support for the Palestinians against Israel; and on November 4, the event to mark thirty years since the occupation of the US embassy in 1979. The number of arrests and prisoners in custody grew. Through the summer and autumn ugly stories spread of the torture and death of protestors in custody, and estimates of the number of deaths mounted to several hundred.

On December 19, 2009, Hosein-Ali Montazeri, the senior cleric most associated with the reform movement, died in his sleep at the age of eighty-seven. There were further demonstrations associated with his funeral in Qom on December 21, and pro-regime thugs attacked Mousavi and Karrubi (the other reformist candidate at the June elections) there in the street. There were more demonstrations on December 27, the day of Ashura. On February 11, 2010 (the anniversary of the final triumph of the revolution in 1979), the regime countered the opposition's practice of using familiar dates in the calendar to take over official events by flooding the streets with police and basij, closing down Internet servers and mobile-phone networks, and by closing off access to Azadi Square by all but pro-regime supporters bused in from outside. The demonstrators tried again on February 14, 2011, but again had no answer to the regime's tactics. That attempt was effectively the last. The hard-line leadership took Mousavi and Karrubi into house arrest, where they remain at the time of writing (August 2016). Large numbers of reformists left the country and went into exile after June 2009, and an unknown further number are still in prison.

In June 2015 a poll was carried out in Iran about the events of 2009 and attitudes to the Green Movement. One has to be cautious about all polling, and especially polling within Iran (where those polled may often have real concerns about anonymity) but the results are nonetheless of interest. Of those polled, 59 percent said that they believed the results of the 2009 election had been accurate and no fraud had taken place; 19 percent said there had been fraud by the government, and 22 percent said they didn't know or could not comment. The poll also indicated that better-educated, urban Iranians were more likely to doubt the outcome of the elections; and it found that exactly the same proportion of those polled (28 percent in each case) used the term "Green Movement" as used the term "Sedition" (the Iranian government's term for those who demonstrated against the 2009 election result). However skeptical one may be from outside Iran, one must accept that a significant proportion of Iranians, perhaps a majority, believe that the outcome of the election was valid. The election produced, or reflected, among other things, a division in Iranian society itself.

At the time, some western commentators said or wrote that the outcome of the elections was immaterial because there was little to choose between the policy intentions of the two main protagonists, Mousavi and Ahmadinejad. That missed the point. Mousavi and his reformist supporters were not looking to overturn the Islamic Republic, but what had happened was no less important for the fact that they were not following a western-inspired agenda. By falsifying the election results (as was widely believed to have happened), the regime had gone much further than ever before in subverting the representative element in the Iranian constitution and—irrespective of what really was or was not done with the election results—had precipitated a crisis over the very nature of the Islamic Republic. Important figures like former presidents Rafsanjani and Khatami were openly critical of what had happened. The opposition candidates Mousavi and Karrubi refused to shut up. Several leading clerics were critical of the conduct of the elections, and others stayed pointedly silent. The crisis was not just a confrontation between the regime and a section of the populace; it was also a crisis within the regime. The Supreme Leader Ali Khamenei was forced to take a more partisan position than ever before, abandoning the notion that his office put him above day-to-day politics; and he became more dependent on the support of the Revolutionary Guard (Sepah).

How important is the Revolutionary Guard (Sepah) in Iranian politics?

Iran's Revolutionary Guard Corps (Sepah-e Pasdaran-e Enqelab-e Eslami)—called Sepah for short by most Iranians—was established in 1979 as a paramilitary force to protect the revolutionary government, answerable directly to Khomeini. In its early history it was tasked with fighting Kurdish separatists and the Mojahedin-e Khalq Organisation (MKO, but-grew rapidly and was transformed above all by the conflict with Iraq. The tendency of regime propaganda then and since has been to credit the Sepah with most of the success in the fighting against Saddam's forces; but the Sepah were indeed crucial in the fighting at many decisive points, and their units often suffered very heavy casualties—notably in the Karbala 4 and Karbala 5 offensives in the winter of 1986–1987 but on many other occasions also.

Khomeini was clear that the Sepah should not take an active part in politics, but their constitutional responsibility for protecting the Islamic Republic against internal as well as external threats left a gray area for interpretation, and in the years since Khomeini's death they have taken a larger and larger role in many aspects of life in Iran. In the summer of 1999 a group of Sepah commanders sent a letter to President Khatami, warning him that if the government did not take action against student demonstrations in Tehran, then the Sepah would have to step in. This did not happen, but their role in facing down the demonstrations in the aftermath of the elections of 2009 (and Khamenei's dependence on them) strengthened the position of the Sepah within the system. Their close relationship with Ahmadinejad was well known, and he intervened frequently to support their interests, especially in the construction sector, both as president and previously when he was mayor of Tehran. The role of the Revolutionary Guard in the economy was emphasized further in October 2009 when a company linked to the Revolutionary Guards paid the equivalent of nearly US$8 billion for a controlling share in the state telecommunications monopoly. As sanctions intensified after the autumn of 2011, many observers suggested that the Sepah benefited disproportionately from smuggling and sanctions-busting operations, though such allegations are of course difficult to prove.

The Sepah has taken an ever-greater role within the Iranian system, but as in other parts of the system, there is a plurality opinion; one reflection of this is the fact that the former commander of the Sepah, Mohsen Rezai, stood against Ahmadinejad in the presidential election of 2009; and when Khamenei and Ahmadinejad ultimately fell out, the Sepah sided with Khamenei rather than the cheeky challenger. The Sepah commanders have an important voice in debates within the Supreme National Security

Council (SNSC) and the system generally, but not necessarily a dominant one, and decision making is collegiate.
Khamenei is dependent on them, but they also depend on
him, and on the principle of *velayat-e faqih*, for such authority as they have. It is not inconceivable that the Sepah, or a
rogue Sepah commander, could one day intervene to rule in
Iran directly, but the Islamic Republic's military tradition is
different from that of Turkey or Egypt, for example—there
is no comparable tradition of military coups or military
rule—and such a move would be a direct contravention of
the principles that have held sway since 1979.

The Sepah has a dual significance for Iranians, reflecting divisions in political opinion in the country. They are
still regarded as heroes of the Iran-Iraq war and guaran-
tors of Iran's independence by many, but also as diehard,
repressive, and sometimes corrupt enforcers of the most
hard-line aspects of the Islamic Republic by others.

Is the Leader, Ali Khamenei, a dictator? Who really runs the Islamic Republic?

As we have seen already, the constitution of the Islamic
Republic includes a variety of different power centers. It
has many of the features of a western-style democracy—
an elected president and Parliament, a judiciary, a government and ministers with ministerial portfolios, and so on.
But these organs of government do not always function in
the way one might expect.

One way to interpret the Iranian constitution is to say
that it seeks to satisfy two principles; the idea of Islamic
government, and the idea of popular sovereignty. Of the
two, the Islamic principle is the dominant one in the actual
text of the constitution. By contrast, details of the way the
president and the Parliament should be elected are set out
clearly, but no principle of popular sovereignty is directly

stated. Popular sovereignty is implicit rather than explicit in the text. The supremacy of the Islamic principle over the democratic principle has also been evident in the conduct of politics since 1979; but despite all the constraints, limitations, and abuses, representative politics has nonetheless contributed significantly to the shaping of events.

The prime repository of Islamic authority under the constitution is the *rahbar* (Leader)—currently Ali Khamenei. He is often called Supreme Leader in western publications, and that term is used in Iran too (*rahbar-e moazzam*), but the constitution itself uses only the term *rahbar*. The Leader has the ultimate authority in the state; he appoints the heads of the armed services, including the Sepah, and also the judiciary. The president and the Parliament (Majles) are elected, but crucially the candidates for elections have to be vetted for approval beforehand by the Guardian Council, which again is effectively controlled by the Leader (it has twelve members, six of whom are appointed by the Leader directly, with the remaining six chosen by the judiciary— but the judiciary themselves are chosen by the Leader). The vetting process is brutal; usually a majority of those who put themselves forward as candidates are rejected by the Guardian Council—in presidential elections, only a tiny minority of those who put themselves forward are allowed to stand. The Leader also appoints Friday Prayer Leaders, the head of the Basij militia, and the head of the state broadcasting organization, and censorship of the media is enforced by the judiciary and the Ministry of Islamic Guidance, but the Guardian Council is the prime means by which he and the circle of advisers around him manipulate the democratic element in the system.

Despite the sweeping nature of the Leader's powers, the system (*nezam*) does not operate like a dictatorship as such—even in Khomeini's time this was not the case. Khamenei leaves the day-to-day operation of government to the president and his ministers, and major decisions are taken only after consultation; both within his own circle of advisers and (for major decisions bearing upon foreign and defense policy) within the SNSC, of which he is the chairman. The SNSC includes the president, foreign minister, all the heads of the armed services, and the head of the Sepah. The president has a limited role within the system, and whenever presidents have tried to resist the power of the Leader in the past, or to carve out a separate power base for themselves, the Leader has eventually been able to make them back down.

Far from calling Iran a dictatorship, sometimes critics suggest almost the opposite; that the system is a chaotic confusion of power centers—Sepah, president, Intelligence Ministry, army, Supreme Leader, Guardian Council—competing for influence and taking action independently. This is sometimes used to explain alleged Iranian support for terrorism or for insurgent groups in other countries. In the early years after the revolution, the picture of chaotically competing power centers within Iran was more accurate; Khomeini exploited that disorder to consolidate the Islamic Republic. Today, many of those power centers are still there, but the Iranian system has matured, and none of them is out of control. The SNSC is the prime organ of the state to ensure a central grip on policy, and to ensure that the authority of the state and of the Supreme Leader is upheld. There is little or no space left for rogue elements.

Elections still happen. Presidents and parliaments are elected, reflecting popular opinion (albeit imperfectly), replacing personalities in office with new faces, and having an effect on political events. This is significant, and should not be lightly dismissed. But the Leader and his circle have the last word, in the interests of Islam and (above all) the maintenance of the *nezam*, and it is not a full democracy.

One could call it a paternalistic Islamic subdemocracy—or an Islamic Republic.

What was the significance of Rouhani's election as president in 2013?

Given the continuing constraints on dissent and the continuing atmosphere of what observers called securitization (control of the press, political activity, movement in and out of the country, and so on by the Intelligence Ministry and other bodies), in the run-up to the presidential election of June 2013 the safe prediction seemed to be that it would follow the pattern of 2009, with manipulation of the process at whatever level necessary to secure the election of a candidate aligned with the Leader and his circle. This expectation seemed to be confirmed when the candidates' list was vetted in May to exclude Rafsanjani. This was a shock—for the former president to be vetoed by the Guardian Council seemed to emphasize yet again the degree to which the system had lurched to the right. Rafsanjani was, seemingly, being punished for his critical statements in the aftermath of the 2009 elections.

This was not the only way in which the list of candidates was interesting, however. Ahmadinejad's favored candidate was also excluded; a final snub to him. The Guardian Council approved eight presidential candidates, of whom five were hard-line conservatives (Jalili, Qalibaf, Rezai, Velayati, Haddad-Adel), one was a moderate conservative (Rouhani) and two were reformists (Aref and Gharazi). It did not look too exciting; Qalibaf, Velayati, and Rezai had all lost in previous presidential elections, Aref and Gharazi were not well known, and Rouhani, while familiar as a diplomat, had not previously campaigned as a politician. But three of the candidates had serious foreign policy experience (Velayati, Rouhani, and Jalili), indicating even at this early stage that the regime wanted to find a president who could solve the nuclear problem and secure relief from sanctions.

The crisis over the economy, sanctions, and the nuclear program dominated the election campaign. Jalili, who had been the chief nuclear negotiator under Ahmadinejad, appeared at first to be the preferred regime candidate. But in one highly significant moment in the debates Velayati (of all the candidates perhaps the one closest to Khamenei himself) criticized Jalili's conduct of the nuclear negotiations for being excessively obstructive and unimaginative—an unprecedented public display of disagreement within the highest circles of the system—and another indication that policy was shifting.

As the campaign went forward Aref and Haddad-Adel dropped out. Rouhani tried to present himself as a candidate not just for moderates and those who might have voted for Rafsanjani, his core base of support, but for more reformist-minded voters also. He gathered support from reformists for his statements in favor of female equality, release of political prisoners, and free speech. His efforts were boosted enormously when Khatami gave him his endorsement shortly before the poll on June 14.

When the votes were counted, the results showed that Rouhani had been elected with 50.7 percent of the vote—just past the 50 percent threshold for a candidate to succeed without a second voting round. He was well ahead of his nearest rival, Mohammad Qalibaf, with more than three times the number of votes.

If one believes that the 2009 election was a fraud, then one could easily accept that it would not have been difficult for the leadership circle to skew the 2013 result by the one or two percentage points necessary to ensure that the voting went to a second round—and it was far from clear that Rouhani would have won a second round. This suggests again the impression that the election implied a decision by Khamenei and his circle in favor of a candidate well placed and well qualified to resolve the nuclear dispute. But Rouhani's election was significant in another way too. As we have seen, Ahmadinejad's controversial presidency had been a shift to the right in Iranian politics. The aftermath of the 2009 elections, irrespective of lingering questions about its legitimacy, unquestionably increased the dependence of the Leader on the Revolutionary Guard and the rest of the security apparatus, and was a dangerous further lurch in the same direction. In his time, Khamenei's role model and the father of the Islamic Republic, Ayatollah Khomeini, always tried to keep left and right in balance. Despite the fact that Khamenei and Ahmadinejad eventually came through, the huge demonstrations that followed the disputed election of 2009—the biggest since the revolution of 1979—must have sounded as a warning to Khamenei. Without running down Rouhani's electoral success in 2013, the result looks also like a deliberate rebalancing of the system; a return toward what one could regard as Khomeini's model of balance and more (relatively) broad-based government. More of the political class were brought back into the tent (though those who had supported what was called the Sedition in 2009 were still excluded).

Why has Iran supported the Assad regime in Syria?

Syria and Iran are in some ways improbable allies. As an Islamic Republic, one might not have expected Iran to ally itself with a dictatorship that grew out of the political doctrine of Baathism: a secular Arab nationalist movement that originated in the 1930s and 1940s. But politics, and perhaps especially the politics of relations between states, develops its own logic, which often has little to do with ideology. Baathism advocated Arab unity, but two of its founding fathers, Michel Aflaq and Zaki al-Arsuzi (both Syrians), disliked each other, and would not be members of the same party. Projects to fuse Syria and Egypt, and later on, Syria and Iraq, both foundered, creating in the latter case a personal bitterness between Hafez al-Assad and Saddam Hussein (despite the fact that both were Baathists, at least nominally) that led to the two states breaking off diplomatic relations altogether at the end of 1979. When Saddam sent his troops to invade Iran the following year, Syria and Iran became allies against Iraq. Syria cut off an oil pipeline that had allowed Iraq to export its oil from a Mediterranean port, and Iran supplied Syria with cheap oil. Iran and Syria had other things in common, including resistance to the United States in the region, opposition to Israel, and a supportive relationship toward the Shi'a Muslims of Lebanon, which led to the creation of Lebanese Hezbollah, with Iranian help, after the Israeli invasion of Lebanon in 1982. Since then Syria has been of value to Iran as a reliable ally, but also as Iran's bridge to Lebanese Hezbollah.

After the revolt against the Assad regime began in the spring of 2011, Iran supported the regime with Sepah advisers, financial support, and (it is believed) at least some troops. Significant numbers of Lebanese Hezbollah fighters have also been present, facilitated by Iran and with Iranian support. When the Assad regime came under intense international pressure in the late summer of 2013 for using chemical weapons, the Iranians under the newly elected President Rouhani were instrumental in inducing the Syrian regime to give up at least some of its remaining stock of those weapons. Around the same time the Iranians seemed to indicate that they might be able to accept an eventual solution to the civil war in Syria that did not involve Hafez al-Assad, but later their position hardened again. There was speculation in 2014 and the early part of 2015, as it began to look more likely that a nuclear deal would be achieved, that the Iranians might be a constructive partner for the west in fighting Daesh/Islamic State in Syria and in finding an eventual settlement, but those hopes receded again after the settlement was achieved in July, and the Iranians appeared reluctant to engage. Then in the autumn, when Assad apparently came close to collapse, the Iranian position of support for him received a boost when the Russians intervened with a much more intensive air campaign.

The Iranians were therefore bound to welcome the Russian intervention; but the history of relations between Iran and Russia is not a happy one, and a greater Russian military presence in the Iranians' near abroad must have made some Iranians uneasy, at least—especially when Russian ships launched cruise missiles from the Caspian Sea that tracked across Iranian territory on their way to targets in Syria in the autumn of 2015 (announcing at the time that this territory was "unoccupied"). Through 2016 Iranian policy drew closer still to Russia, with the revelation in August that Russian warplanes had been operating out of Nozheh airbase, near Hamadan. Multilateral talks on the future of Syria from the end of October 2015, including the Iranians for the first time, showed at least some hope for progress.

How has the position of women changed in Iran since 1979?

The whole question of the status of women in Iran since the revolution of 1979 is shot through with paradox, and (even more than is the case in other areas of Iranian life) it is barely possible to make any strong statement about it without a balancing statement to contrary or near-contrary effect. Yet there is almost no other complex of phenomena so important in understanding contemporary Iran, and important trends for Iran's future.

To begin with, Khomeini's position on the status of women was both highly political and rather changeable. In 1963–1964, when he first came to prominence as an opponent of the Shah, he attacked the Shah's policy of giving women the vote (rather than criticize his plans for land reform, which were popular with peasants but endangered clerical land endowments). But in 1979, recognizing the contribution women had made to the overthrow of the Shah, he did not attempt to turn the clock back and remove women's suffrage. Instead he reimposed the veil and removed liberalizing legislation established by the Shah in the Family Protection Law of 1967, reaffirming the provisions of shari'a law in its place, and the principle of male supremacy in the family. This meant, among other things, that women lost rights of custody over children in the event of divorce, and a woman's evidence in a criminal trial counted for less than a man's. It became impossible for women to serve as judges in law courts, or indeed, for a time, as lawyers at all (this meant that Shirin Ebadi, who years later, in 2003, became Iran's first winner of the Nobel Peace Prize for her work in Iran as a human rights lawyer, and had become Iran's first female judge in 1975, could not practice her profession from 1979 to 1993). Other changes entailed by the removal of the family protection law, however, including the theoretical reestablishment of legal polygamy and reduction of the legal age of marriage for girls to nine years old (later adjusted officially to thirteen), had only a marginal real effect in the long term because of social stigma against such practices.

Many Iranian women, especially but not exclusively those of leftist views who had participated actively in the demonstrations of 1978, felt bitterly betrayed by the changes to women's status that were made in the early months of the new Islamic Republic. Nonetheless, there were other changes afoot that were arguably as important or more important for women in the long run. The effect of the Iran-Iraq war was one factor; women took men's roles in work and in the home when men were away at the front. But changes in education also led to major changes that are often not appreciated outside the Islamic Republic.

Partly because of the high birth rate and rapidly rising population, but also because of his government's bias toward urban development at the expense of rural Iran, the Shah never succeeded in extending universal primary education to the whole country. Under the Islamic Republic even the most remote villages got a school, and within a few years all children could expect to get a basic education. Literacy rates rose quickly and were at 86.8 percent in 2015. At the same time, many families in more conservative rural areas and provincial towns (or rather, fathers of such families) were content for the first time to send their daughters to school, because schools were segregated by gender and girls (from age nine) wore hejab. It became normal for boys and girls to attend school, and such is the underlying cultural respect for learning and intellectual attainment in Iran generally, that many families pushed their children on to get the best qualifications possible, to continue school to age eighteen and go on to university. The government encouraged this too, especially in the years after the Iran-Iraq war when large numbers of new provincial universities and free universities (Azad universities—independent of government funding, financed from student fees) were set up.

At this point a phenomenon familiar from secondary-level education in many western countries intervened—girls in their teenage years in Iran have tended to be more academically diligent and to get better exam results. The upshot of all this has been that girls have done better in university entrance exams, and so for years (since the late 1990s) 60–65 percent of university entrants have been female. In turn these well-qualified young women have left university and have entered the labor market, where many of them have secured good jobs (despite eye-wateringly high youth unemployment levels—higher still for young women). Women are noticeably plentiful in education (over half of teachers in Iran are now women), in clerical positions in the private sector, in medicine, and in the civil service.

One way of looking at the progress in the position of women in Iran is as an outcome of the success of the clergy in securing to themselves the control of politics and policymaking in the country. The clergy are Iran's traditional intelligentsia; if any class of people were likely to regard education as a good in itself, for all, without reservations, it was them. The mass education of women to higher level and their greater presence in the working life of the country are a consequence of that underlying position. The success of women in education has had other consequences; in many families women earn more than their husbands, and better education means more choice in other aspects of life also. On average, women are marrying later, and some well-qualified women look around the marriage market and decide not to marry at all. Some observers have noted the development of more liberal attitudes toward family, work, and politics and have connected this to greater self-confidence and earning power among middle-class women; and others (notably Ziba Mir-Hosseini and Charles Kurzman) have spoken of a feminist generation in Iran.

One should not exaggerate. This is largely a middle-class phenomenon; most lower-class Iranian women cannot even dream of getting well-paid jobs, and instead have to struggle their way forward in conditions dominated by the brute facts of high unemployment, unjust gender discrimination, and poverty, where many lives are irretrievably blighted by drug addiction, prostitution, and family break-down. Women still do not rise to managerial positions in any sector of the economy in significant numbers, and ele-ments within the regime have tried in recent years to set quotas to limit the numbers of women in some university courses (so far, the outcome of their efforts remains un-clear). The unequal treatment in law is a continuing and humiliating blemish on legitimate aspirations for women's equality in Iran.

But the shift in the social position of some Iranian women seems bound to have major long-term effects on Iranian society and politics more generally. In the overall picture, which still has many dark areas, it has to be one of the brighter features that permits a degree of cautious optimism.

How bad are the human rights abuses?

There are serious human rights abuses in Iran. Amnesty International believed that nearly seven hundred people were executed in Iran between January and July 2015 (though the figures were disputed) and, according to some, Iran executes more people per capita than any other coun-try in the world. Amnesty have been particularly con-cerned about the number of executions of juveniles—a consequence of the relatively low age of criminal respon-sibility (fifteen for boys and nine for girls). About three-quarters of the executions are for drug-related offenses, and almost all the rest are for murder and other serious crimes. Freedom of speech and freedom of the media are restricted and there are significant numbers of political prisoners. Journalists, filmmakers, and others are arrested and imprisoned. Conditions in prison are bad; prisoners often contract diseases, and medical treatment for them is often poor and sometimes withheld. Despite being outlawed in the constitution, torture is used in prisons and by the police (it is called punishment rather than torture).

Traditional Islamic punishments like stoning for adultery and amputation of limbs for theft are sometimes applied, but less frequently in recent years due to public disapproval within Iran, pressure from the regime, and international pressure from outside. One aspect of this is the continuing division within the legal system in Iran. On the one hand, there is the legal code and the official court system, which operate more or less in the same way to that in many countries, albeit with shortcomings and abuses, failures to observe due process, proper provision for defense counsel, and so on. On the other hand, especially in provincial districts, clerics may deliver judgments according to shari'a law independently of the official legal system. Many (perhaps most) of these judgments may be reasonable and humane, but others are not.

Islam is a religion of law and the Islamic Republic treats offenders harshly partly because Islamic law permits harsh penalties in the hardest cases. The high rate of executions reflects the seriousness of Iran's drug problem (partly caused by the drugs trade to Europe across Iran's borders) and other social problems. Within the Middle East context, Iran's human rights record is not so exceptional, and there are other countries that are worse in many respects. But it would be egregious to make excuses. The record is bad, most of Iran's civilized and well-educated population know it is bad, the regime could improve it relatively easily (without abandoning shari'a principles) and it should do so.

Is Iran the Soviet Union of the twenty-first century?

In a word, no. This suggestion has sometimes surfaced in the media or in other circles in the United States, or in Israel when anti-Iran statements were being made that fell short of even more extreme comparisons that were sometimes made with Nazi Germany. Iran is not a threat to the West in any way that can sensibly be compared with the threat that used to be posed by the Soviet Union—and in addition, there are now threats to western interests from elsewhere in the Middle East that are plainly more serious than any threat from Iran, especially after the nuclear settlement of July 2015. With or without nuclear weapons, Iran will never have the global strategic reach of the former Soviet Union, nor the offensive military power in conventional forces to back it up, nor the defense spending, nor the military-industrial complex. Nor the military occupation of half a continent. Nor the totalizing grip on the thought of its own population.

Iran's military spending is relatively low by comparison with its neighbors. As a share of gross domestic product (GDP), Iran's figure for military spending was 2.3 percent in 2012, the most recent year for which figures were available at the time of writing (though this figure, drawn from assessments made by the Stockholm International Peace Research Institute as of November 2015, may not include spending on the Sepah, which could lift the figure by around another 0.5 to 0.75 of a percentage point). By comparison, the equivalent figure for Saudi Arabia in the same year was 7.7 percent (up to 10.4 percent in 2014); for Israel, 5.7 percent; and for the United Arab Emirates, 4.8 percent. In the same year the figure for the United States was 4.2 percent. To refer back to the Soviet comparator, it has been estimated that Soviet defense spending was around 15 to 17 percent in the mid-1980s. By no measure is Iran among the leaders in regional or world defense spending. If defense spending is any measure of militarism, or a sign of expansionist intent, then Iran is not a militaristic or expansionist state.

In addition, where the Soviet Union represented an ideology that was persuasive to some within western societies, and stood for one side of a debate or conflict within western democracy itself, Iran's Islamic ideology has no such purchase within western society (and less than one might think even in the Middle East). Some might argue that Islamists are indeed active in western society, but they are active largely within communities of Muslims, mainly immigrants. The general appeal of their views is limited and small; their views do not form one end of a continuum of political debate as Soviet-aligned communism in western society used to do. Moreover, those who are most active and most dangerous are Wahhabi or Salafi Sunnis, deriving their support from Saudi Arabia and other Arab states from the southern shore of the Persian Gulf, not Shi'as influenced by Iran. Iran's attachment to the minority, Shi'a side of the Muslim schism further limits its ideological reach; only around 12 percent of the world's Muslims are Shi'a.

Does Iran, like the former Soviet Union, interfere in neighboring countries and attempt to spread its revolution? Yes ... and no. The present regimes in Afghanistan and Iraq, perhaps best called proto-democratic and supported by the United States and the West, are pro-Iranian and were set up with Iranian help. In both places Iran has supported the same groups and personalities that the West supported. Iranian involvement in insurgency in Iraq became something of a chestnut between 2003 and 2009 as some tried to blame Iran for the western coalition's difficulties; but there was much more evidence for the destabilizing effect of support for insurgency originating in Saudi Arabia, which tended to be ignored. A similar pattern emerged later, in Afghanistan. For the most part, Iranian rhetoric about exporting revolution did not survive the earlier phases of the Iran-Iraq war, and the Shi'a crescent theory, of a threat of Iranian-backed revolt by the Shi'a underclasses of the Persian Gulf region, has been shown to be bunk (notably by the French academic

Laurence Louër). Iran has interests and associates in both Iraq and Afghanistan, and the interests, like the borders, are permanent (unlike, perhaps, those of the United States and its allies). The closer to Iran's borders, the more pragmatic Iran's foreign and security policy has been. Since the emergence of Daesh/Islamic State in Iraq in the summer of 2014, Iranian support for the Shi'as of southern Iraq has strengthened and has emerged more fully into plain sight. But the stated Iranian policy toward both Iraq and Afghanistan has been to foster stability in both (for, from an Iranian perspective, eminently cogent reasons), and it is a serious failure of western *and* Iranian diplomacy that we and they have been unable to make better use of the strong alignment of interests between ourselves. In many nearby countries with Shi'a minorities (or majorities in the cases of Iraq and Bahrain) Iran and Iranian clerics have relationships with those communities. But those relationships are not relationships of control; at most they are of support for self-defense. Iran's relationship with Lebanese Hezbollah is exceptional because of Hezbollah's proximity to Israel and Iran's hostility toward Israel, but even there Hezbollah's posture has been largely defensive, notwithstanding the rhetoric.

Turning to the conduct of the regime internally, comparison between Iran and the former Soviet Union may be a better fit. Opposition to the United States is still a fundamental ideological position of the Iranian regime, even after the nuclear deal in the summer of 2015, and the enmity and supposed interference of the United States is still used to justify internal repression. As in the former Soviet Union, the ideology has become fatigued and the ruling clique increasingly (especially since 2009) has used its security apparatus to uphold its dwindling authority. There are other similarities. In his book *Living in Truth* Vaclav Havel described the debilitating effect of living in a society like that of Czechoslovakia under communism, in which dishonesty and lies were necessary for survival and essential for preferment, entering the soul and creating a kind of moral anomie. Azar Nafisi (author of *Reading Lolita in Tehran*) and Ramita Navai (*City of Lies*) have described a similar effect in the Islamic Republic, where the dishonest nature of the regime and compromise with it is made more dismal by the unemployment that keeps many Iranians, especially young Iranians, in a limbo of desperate inactivity and disappointed ambitions, and induces others to make a soul-destroying deal with the regime.

How did the deal made in Vienna in July 2015 over Iran's nuclear program come about, and is it going to hold?

Rouhani's election as president in June 2013 raised expectations that Iran would pursue a resolution of the nuclear dispute with new urgency. When Rouhani went to New York for the UN General Assembly (UNGA) in September, accompanied by his new foreign minister, Mohammad Javad Zarif, American and British spokesmen were soon welcoming a new, more conciliatory and workmanlike approach from the Iranian side. When the politicians and diplomats left New York after the UNGA, Rouhani and Obama spoke to each other in a telephone call—the first such exchange since 1979. After the telephone call and over the course of the negotiations on the nuclear question that followed, diehard hard-liners in Iran criticized what Rouhani was doing, but much more important were the continuing statements from Khamenei in Rouhani's support. With Khamenei behind him, and a huge mandate from the Iranian people, Rouhani could afford to ignore his opponents for the most part.

After the difficult years under Ahmadinejad, talks resumed between Iran and the P5 + 1 (the permanent five of the UN Security Council—the United States, Britain, France, Russia, and China, plus Germany) in October 2013 in a much more positive spirit. When the negotiators met again in Geneva a month later, they succeeded in making a provisional agreement (on November 24). Iran agreed to suspend uranium enrichment above the 5 percent level, in exchange for a relaxation of some sanctions that was worth about $7 billion to Iran (described as "modest" by the US side). The Iranians also agreed to begin converting uranium enriched to a higher level to make it unusable for weapon purposes, to accept a more stringent inspection regime, to cease work on the Arak plutonium plant, and to halt development of improved centrifuges.

Although it was only an interim settlement, it was widely welcomed—not least by Ali Khamenei, who quickly issued a statement saying "God's grace and the support of the Iranian nation were the reasons behind this success." There was opposition from Israel, and from Saudi Arabia, and from within the US Congress, but Obama and his colleagues persevered despite those opposing voices, presenting the deal as a first step toward halting and reversing the Iranian nuclear program.

Perhaps the most important aspect of the deal was that the United States and Iran had looked over the edge of the cliff, at what would follow from continued confrontation and escalation, had pulled back, and had decided to talk instead. The Iranians could have continued with a policy of obfuscation, resisting any kind of constraint on their nuclear program, accepting the price of isolation and the economic damage from sanctions. The United States could have maintained the policy of no enrichment for Iran, as under the Bush administration, as Netanyahu continued to urge from the sidelines, steadily increasing the sanctions pressure until the only remaining option was military force. But Obama pulled back from that course, and took a chance on trusting the Iranians. That was the real significance of the Geneva agreement, and the negotiations that followed. In fact, it emerged later that there had been direct bilateral talks in secret between the Iranians and the United States since March 2013—well before Rouhani had been elected as president.

Under the terms of the Geneva deal, negotiations toward a final settlement were meant to conclude within six months. But it took longer. The involvement of the other state parties was important, but in its essentials it was a US-Iran negotiation. As with all initiatives involving a commitment of this kind, momentum and the political capital invested in the process counted for as much as the technical details. The deadline was postponed twice, in June and November 2014, before a framework deal was agreed on April 2, 2015, and a definitive agreement was finally made in Vienna on July 14: the Joint Comprehensive Plan of Action (JPCOA).

The JPCOA committed Iran to enrich no uranium beyond the level of 3.67 percent and to limit stocks enriched to that level to a maximum of 300 kilograms (for fifteen years), to reduce its number of operational centrifuges from twenty thousand down to under six thousand, and to restrict research and development of more efficient centrifuges (for thirteen years). Other provisions were to convert the underground Fordow plant to medical research with a moratorium on enrichment there for fifteen years, to redesign the Arak plant to prevent production of plutonium, to accept more or less continuous supervision of existing sites, and access to other facilities on request. The lifting of sanctions would be gradual and would depend on fulfillment of the Iranians' obligations.

Although it was adopted by the UN Security Council within a few days, the agreement was met with a storm of criticism from Republicans within the US political system.

Much of this hostility was based on an assumption that Iran was incorrigibly malevolent and untrustworthy. More considered objections to the details of the agreement were augmented by a deep-seated conservative mistrust of arms control measures on principle, the visceral dislike of Iran that had endured since 1979, and an unwillingness to allow the Obama administration a policy success. Eventually opposition in Congress collapsed as it became clear that Obama's opponents would not be able to assemble the votes necessary to overrule a presidential veto, but widespread dislike of the agreement remained.

There were potential problems and renewed concern in the autumn of 2015 over Iran's ballistic missile program, but in practice, the Iranian side met the commitments under the JCPOA that were necessary for the implementation of sanctions relief to begin, and implementation began rather faster than anyone had anticipated. Implementation of sanctions relief went ahead on January 16, 2016, after the International Atomic Energy Agency confirmed that Iran had met the necessary conditions.

The JCPOA was possible only because the leaders of the United States and Iran, the prime parties involved, had both made a huge political investment in it. The working assumption must be that the agreement will continue to hold as long as that commitment remains strong. Within Iran, the successes of moderates and reformists associated with Rouhani in the elections of February 2016 were interpreted as a strong endorsement of the JCPOA by the Iranian people.

How important is the confrontation between Iran and Saudi Arabia, and between Sunni and Shi'a?

After the revolution of 1979 Khomeini railed against several leaders in the Arab world—notably the king of Saudi

Arabia, and also Saddam Hussein in Iraq—but did so because he regarded them as ungodly and (in the Saudi case) because they were allied with the United States, not because they were Sunni. His Shi'ism took a relatively moderate form, at least in terms of the traditional schism between Sunni and Shi'a, and the Islamic Republic tended to frown on the more extreme Shi'a traditions that were most offensive to Sunni Muslims (notably the ritual cursing of the first three Sunni caliphs). In the earliest phase of the revolution Khomeini and other Iranian revolutionaries repeatedly urged Muslims, Sunni or Shi'a, in other countries to rise up against their rulers and create their own Islamic governments, as the Iranians had done.

But Khomeini's direct influence in the Islamic world outside Iran was never great, because for Sunni Muslims he represented Shi'a Iran. More than 85 percent of the world's Muslims are Sunni and many Sunnis have traditionally distrusted and disliked Shi'as. The Islamic revolution had a major effect in the Islamic world outside Iran, but for the most part it was indirect. One aspect of the Iranian revolution was the desire to explode the idea, standard up to that time, that the third world in general and the Middle East in particular would progress on a western model, pushing aside Islam like an outmoded, medieval hangover, toward greater material prosperity and (perhaps) western systems of government. Elsewhere in the Islamic world, some Sunni Muslims, discontented with their own secular-minded, materialistic, western-inclined rulers, were receptive to that message. They were not open to Iranian leadership, but may in some sense have been shamed by the Iranian example; Sunni Islam was for them the correct, rightful form of Islam, but it had been the Shi'a tradition that had stood up first against impiety and western cultural encroachment. So some pious Sunnis felt the need to do something too.

The first demonstration of this mood in Sunni Islam came early and was explosive. On November 20, 1979, just ten months after the final victory of Khomeini and his followers in Iran, a Sunni radical called Juhayman Al-Otaybi occupied the Grand Mosque in Mecca with two hundred to three hundred armed supporters. They criticized the al-Saud family for corruption and for being too open to western influence, and criticized Saudi clerics for not speaking up against these evils. Juhayman demanded that television should be banned, that non-Muslims should be expelled from Saudi Arabia, that Muslims should depose their corrupt leaders, and that there should be a return to the way of life and the example of the Prophet. After the occupation, Juhayman and his supporters were besieged by Saudi security forces for two weeks until they were finally overwhelmed (allegedly with help from outside the country) at the beginning of December. He was executed by beheading with most of his surviving followers a few weeks later.

The Saudi monarchy had suffered a major and embarrassing scare. Saudi Arabia had originally been established on the basis of a pact between the al-Saud family and the puritanical, reforming scholar and preacher, Mohammad ibn Abd al-Wahhab, who lived in the eighteenth century and died in 1792. The version of Sunni Islam preached by Abd al-Wahhab was fundamentalist, puritanical, and harsh, emphasizing monotheism (*tawhid*) and the rejection of innovation (*bid'a*) and idolatry (*shirk*). When the modern state of Saudi Arabia was established after the First World War, Wahhabism (its adherents sometimes prefer the term Salafism) was established with it as the dominant clerical doctrine—strongly hostile to other Muslim traditions like Shi'ism or Sufism, with their veneration of saints, shrines, and tombs, and their greater openness to nonscriptural elements like philosophy and mysticism in religious thinking. For some Saudis, brought up in the Wahhabi tradition,

Juhayman's action in occupying the holy center of Islam in Mecca felt like a prod to a guilty conscience. The al-Saud family were vulnerable to accusations that they had been backsliding on their own basic values.

The Saudi King Khalid's solution was less to combat religious extremism but rather to preempt further dissent and insurrection by appeasing and embracing it, turning the country away from western models (at least on the surface) and back to the harsh principles of Wahhabism. On a superficial level, dress codes were revised; western clothing was abandoned, men and women went back to traditional robes and hijab, and cinemas were closed. But more importantly, the Wahhabi clergy were given a greater role in government, especially in education, and teaching took a more traditional turn. And the government stepped up its support and funding for the preaching of Wahhabism in other Islamic countries around the world, building mosques and schools, in order to counter the supposed threat from Khomeini's Iran (the 1979 crisis had been made worse by a Shi'a rising in the eastern Saudi province of Qatif, just after Juhayman's occupation of the Grand Mosque began—prompted by police repression and a ban on Shi'a ritual processions as well as by the rhetoric emanating from Tehran).

Since 1979 relations between Saudi Arabia and Iran have been a roller-coaster of highs and lows. But across the Islamic world the advance of Saudi-funded Wahhabism has been inexorable, with more intolerant Wahhabism supplanting moderate local traditions in many countries.

Part of the attitude of the Saudis derives from Wahhabism, but another aspect of their traditional distaste for Shi'as, shared by some other Sunni ruling elites in the Arab world, derives from traditional social and political patterns in the region. Before 1918 the Ottomans used regional Sunni elites to enforce their authority in the provinces of their sprawling empire. After the Empire and the Sunni caliphate came to an end after 1918, those traditional Sunni elites continued to wield influence in much of the former Ottoman territory, albeit under the authority of new colonial governments. Even when imperial governments disappeared and Arab nationalism became a renewed political force after the Second World War, most of the new, secular nationalists ruling in places like Egypt and Iraq came from Sunni origins; Saddam Hussein was typical. Sunnis tended to think of themselves as the natural rulers in the region.

Saddam's removal in 2003, and his replacement by a democratically elected, Shi'a-led government, was a shock to Sunnis: especially to the Gulf monarchies, whose Sunni elites may not have liked Saddam, but liked the Shi'a even less, and saw any improvement in the position of the Shi'a as a front for the regional advance of Iran. Politically immature pro-Shi'a partisanship in the conduct of government by Nouri al-Maliki in Iraq after his election as prime minister in 2006 worsened the situation and made Iraqi Sunnis feel even more marginalized, after many of them had been ejected from the army and government by the US-led coalition. The humiliation of the Sunnis in Iraq and the spread of Wahhabi ideology led to support for Al-Qaeda in Iraq and a spate of suicide bombings against Shi'a targets, notably the Shi'a shrines in Iraq. One of the earliest hit the shrine of Ali in Najaf in August 2003—all the other main shrines in Iraq have been targeted repeatedly. One of the most provocative was the destruction of the dome of the shrine at Samarra in February 2006; large numbers of Shi'as were also killed in suicide and car bombings. Shi'as responded in 2004–2005 with large-scale killings of Sunnis by militia death squads.

Sectarian conflict burgeoned until brought under control after the US troop surge in 2007. But Sunni groups who had been encouraged to turn against Al-Qaeda by the coalition later felt abandoned, and still deeply hostile to the Maliki government, creating the conditions for the rise of Daesh/Islamic State, whose leaders made use of the civil war in Syria following the Arab Spring to develop their organization and its tactics before their breakthrough with the taking of Mosul in May 2014. As with the Sunni insurgency before 2007, Daesh/Islamic State have drawn in recruits from around the region and beyond it, but large numbers from Saudi Arabia. Whatever the level of support from within Saudi Arabia for Islamic State/Daesh, it is clear that the Saudi government supported other Sunni groups in Syria fighting the Assad regime, including the Al-Qaeda offshoot the Al-Nusra front, in order to hit back against Iran.

A further escalation took place at the beginning of 2016, after the Saudis executed Sheikh Nimr al-Nimr, a leading dissident Shi'a cleric. Sheikh al-Nimr had supported demonstrations against mistreatment of the Shi'a minority in Saudi Arabia and had spoken in strong terms for the overthrow of the monarchy, but he had not committed or incited violent acts and had tried to distance himself from Iran, as have other Saudi Shi'a leaders. The other forty-six execution victims who died at the same time as Sheikh Nimr al-Nimr were mostly Wahhabi extremists guilty of terrorist acts. Nimr al-Nimr had to die because Wahhabi opinion still had to be appeased; the al-Saud family know that the greatest threat to their retention of power in Saudi Arabia is from their own homegrown and, to a large extent, self-inflicted Wahhabi extremist problem.

Neither side in the Iran-Saudi confrontation has anything like a monopoly of virtue. There is fault on both sides. But for the most part the regime has distanced itself from the Shi'a extremism of the past. There is nothing on the Iranian or Shi'a side damaging enough to rank as an equivalent to the fostering of the Wahhabi worldview that has perpetrated the events of 9/11 and the crimes of Islamic State/Daesh. Iranian policy since at least the end of the Iran-Iraq war has been essentially defensive—with the partial exception of its self-defeating stance toward Israel, which is made more serious by the Iranian Revolutionary Guards' relationship with Lebanese Hezbollah and by intermittent but egregious anti-Zionist outbursts that verge on anti-Semitism.

Saudi Arabia and Iran are both pursuing policies underpinned by fear and insecurity. The Iranians look at the map and see themselves encircled, both by anti-Shi'a Sunni states, and by the United States and other western allies, who until recently were talking about regime change and in their public rhetoric still tend to follow and appease a Saudi account of regional tension. For many Iranians their view of the world is heavily influenced by their experience of the bloody Iran-Iraq war of 1980–1988, which they fought in isolation against a similar constellation of overt and covert enemies. The Saudis and other Gulf Arabs fear Iran partly from a justified resentment at past Iranian rhetoric, but also because they know the fragility of their own grip on power: ruling rentier states dependent on oil money to keep subject populations docile, with armed forces of doubtful effectiveness, and terrified by extremists their own policies helped to create. Unfortunately the uncertainty and to some extent the paranoia of both Saudi Arabia and Iran has led to an escalation of hostility and the development of alliances with powers beyond the region toward a situation where two blocs confront each other in the Middle East. That is a potentially disastrous situation— for Syria and Yemen the disaster has already happened. Those external powers need to reconsider their motives and their real interests in the region. For countries like the United Kingdom a real commitment to regional stability would necessitate giving the Saudis and other Gulf States some hard messages that in the past have been thought incompatible with what David Cameron's government and the UK Treasury called the Prosperity Agenda.

The tension between Saudi Arabia and Iran has already contributed to terrible suffering in countries like Iraq, Syria, Bahrain, and Yemen; it is highly desirable that it should be defused. Some form of diplomatic rapprochement between Iran and Saudi Arabia is possible (along the lines of what was achieved in Khatami's time), perhaps even likely; but the tension will be hard to remove entirely, given that the roots of it run so deep.

What are the prospects for Iran after the nuclear agreement of 2015?

The lifting of nuclear-related sanctions in January 2016 was followed (and preceded in some cases) by a surge of interest from outside in the commercial opportunities offered by the Iranian economy. Within a few days a deal was announced for Iran to buy 114 Airbus aircraft, and other similar announcements followed quickly, with Italian and French companies leading the way, despite lingering concerns over the ability of Iranian banks to satisfy the world banking system's requirements over money laundering and other related regulatory matters, and concerns about the effect of continuing sanctions by regimes related to ballistic missiles and human rights.

The widely held perception was that Iran had huge, relatively untapped, and undervalued economic potential. Years of sanctions had artificially depressed economic activity, the value of the Iranian national currency, and the value of Iranian assets and businesses. In addition, Iran owned the world's fourth largest oil reserves and the world's largest natural gas reserves. It also had a highly educated population (a literacy rate of 86 percent) and a strong entrepreneurial tradition, which had combined in recent years to produce, for example, a number of innovative businesses in the IT sector. High youth unemployment meant a pool of cheap labor, ready to take advantage of jobs released by new investment. Iran's diaspora of four to five million people were also a resource (an estimated five hundred thousand in California alone); many of those Iranians had cutting-edge businesses in western economies; some of them traveled back frequently and were ready to invest money and know-how back home, given favorable conditions.

But set against that were a number of less encouraging factors. The economy had been depressed partly due to the effect of sanctions, but also because of poor economic planning, still marked by a statist mindset. The dominance of hydrocarbons in the economy and the related insidious effects of rentierism also acted as a brake; there were concerns about legal safeguards for commercial activity, especially by foreigners; and it remained to be seen how the Revolutionary Guards would manage their commercial interests in the new circumstances. Corruption was a widespread problem; the monitoring organization Transparency International rated Iran 130th out of 168 worldwide in 2015 (with Denmark in first position and Somalia and North Korea sharing 167th place). Many of these problems could be expected to be ironed out as Iran reintegrated into the international system, but some of the pioneers would be likely to get a bumpy ride, and as 2016 drew on, there was increasing unease among Iranians that the economic benefits of the JCPOA had not yet arrived on the tables of ordinary people.

More broadly, as we have seen, it was also a mixed picture. The promise of a more open society under Rouhani seemed slow to materialize; constraints on media freedom remained in force. The opposition leaders of 2009, Mir-Hosein Mousavi and Mehdi Karrubi, remained under house arrest, as did the filmmaker Jafar Panahi. In March 2016 Shirin Ebadi, another of Iran's most distinguished figures, forced into exile in 2009, criticized the nuclear deal for failing to include a human rights dimension. On March 9 the Revolutionary Guards tested two missiles, which, according to Fars News, were adorned with the message "Israel must be wiped out." As one part of the country opened up to the outside world, another chose to broadcast its continuing commitment to slogans from the revolutionary past. It seems likely that Iran will continue to be pulled in two incompatible directions for some time to come.

FURTHER READING

Abrahamian, Ervand. *Iran Between Two Revolutions*, Princeton 1982.

Abrahamian, Ervand. *Radical Islam: The Iranian Mojahedin*, London 1989.

Abrahamian, Ervand. *Khomeinism: Essays on the Islamic Republic*, Berkeley 1993.

Abrahamian, Ervand. *Tortured Confessions: Prisons and Public Recantations in Modern Iran*, Berkeley 1999.

Abrahamian, Ervand. *A History of Modern Iran*, Cambridge 2009.

Afshari, Reza. "The Discourse and Practice of Human Rights Violations of Iranian Baha'is in the Islamic Republic of Iran" in *The Baha'is of Iran: Socio-historical studies*, ed. Dominic Parviz Brookshaw and Seena B. Fazel, Abingdon 2008, 232–277.

Aghaie, Kamran Scot. *The Martyrs of Karbala: Shi'i Symbols and Rituals in Modern Iran*, Seattle 2004.

Alam, Asadollah. *The Shah and I: The Confidential Diary of Iran's Royal Court, 1968–1977*, London 2008.

Alavi, Nasrin. *We Are Iran*, London 2005.

Algar, Hamid. "Shi'ism and Iran in the Eighteenth Century" in *Studies in 18th Century Islamic History*, ed. Thomas Naff and Roger Owen, Carbondale and Edwardsville, 1977, 288–302.

Algar, Hamid (ed and trans). *Constitution of the Islamic Republic of Iran*, Berkeley 1980.

Alvandi, Roham. *Nixon, Kissinger and the Shah: The United States and Iran in the Cold War*, New York 2014.

Aminrazavi, Mehdi. *The Wine of Wisdom*, Oxford 2005.

Ansari, Ali. *Modern Iran since 1921*, Harlow 2003.

Ansari, Ali. *Confronting Iran: The Failure of American Foreign Policy and the Roots of Mistrust*, London 2006.

Ansari, Ali. *Crisis of Authority: Iran's 2009 Presidential Election*, London 2010.

Arberry, A. J. *Classical Persian Literature*, London 1958 (reprinted 2004).

Arjomand, Saïd Amir. *The Turban for the Crown: The Islamic Revolution in Iran*, Oxford 1988.

Arjomand, Saïd Amir. *After Khomeini: Iran under His Successors*, Oxford 2009.

Avery, Peter. *Modern Iran*, New York 1965.

Axworthy, Michael. *The Sword of Persia*, London 2006.

Axworthy, Michael. "The Army of Nader Shah" in *Iranian Studies*, vol. 40, no. 5, December 2007, 635–646.

Axworthy, Michael. *Iran: Empire of the Mind*, London 2008.

Axworthy, Michael. *Revolutionary Iran*, London 2013.

Azari, Farah. *Women of Iran: The Conflict with Fundamentalist Islam*, London 1983.

al-Azm, Sadik. "Is the fatwa a fatwa?" in *Middle East Report*, no. 183, July/August 1993, 27.

Babayan, Kathryn. *Mystics, Monarchs and Messiahs: Cultural Landscapes of Early Modern Iran*, Harvard 2002.

Bakhash, Shaul. *The Reign of the Ayatollahs*, London 1986.

Baktiari, Bahman. *Parliamentary Politics in Revolutionary Iran: The Institutionalisation of Factional Politics*, Gainesville 1996.

Bani Sadr, Abol Hasan. *My Turn to Speak*, Washington 1991.

Bausani, Alessandro. *Religion in Iran*, New York 2000.

Bayandor, Darioush. *Iran and the CIA: The Fall of Mosaddeq Revisited*, London 2010.

Beck, Lois. "Women among Qashqai Nomadic Pastoralists in Iran" in *Women in the Muslim World*, ed. N. Keddie, Cambridge, Mass 1978, 351–373.

Behrooz, Maziar. *Rebels with a Cause: The Failure of the Left in Iran*, London 2000.

Bill, James A. *The Eagle and the Lion: The Tragedy of American-Iranian Relations*, Yale 1988.

Bjerre Christensen, Janne. *Drugs, Deviancy and Democracy in Iran: The Interaction of State and Civil Society*, London 2011.

Bowden, Mark. *Guests of the Ayatollah: The Iran Hostage Crisis: The First Battle in America's War with Militant Islam*, New York 2007.

Boyce, Mary. *Zoroastrianism: A Shadowy but Powerful Presence in the Judaeo-Christian World*, London 1987.

Boyle, John Andrew (ed and trans). *The History of the World-Conqueror (Juvayni)*, Manchester 1958.

Briant, Pierre. *From Cyrus to Alexander: A History of the Persian Empire*, Winona Lake 2002.

Brown, Ian. *Khomeini's Forgotten Sons: The Story of Iran's Boy Soldiers: Child Victims of Saddam's Iraq*, London 1990.

Browne, Edward Glanville. *The Persian Revolution of 1905–1909*, London 1966.

Browne, Edward Glanville. *A Literary History of Persia*, Cambridge 1969.

Buchta, Wilfried. *Who Rules Iran?* Washington 2000.

Chehabi, H. E. *Iranian Politics and Religious Modernism: The Liberation Movement of Iran under the Shah and Khomeini*, London 1990.

Chehabi, H. E. "The Banning of the Veil and Its Consequences" in *The Making of Modern Iran: State and Society under Reza Shah, 1921–1941*, ed. Stephanie Cronin, London 2003, 203–221.

Chehabi, H. E. "Iran and Lebanon in the Revolutionary Decade" in *Distant Relations: Iran and Lebanon in the Last 500 Years*, ed. H. E. Chehabi, London 2006, 201–230.

Chehabi, H. E. "Iran and Lebanon after Khomeini" in *Distant Relations: Iran and Lebanon in the Last 500 Years*, ed. H. E. Chehabi, London 2006, 287–308.

Chubin, Shahram and Tripp, Charles. *Iran and Iraq at War*, London 1988.

Cole, Juan R. I. *Sacred Space and Holy War: The Politics, Culture and History of Shi'ite Islam*, London 2002.

Colledge, Malcolm A. R. *The Parthians*, London 1967.

Cooper, Tom and Bishop, Farzad. *Iranian F-14 Tomcat Units in Combat*, Botley 2004.

Corbin, Henry (trans Nancy Pearson). *Spiritual Body and Celestial Earth*, Princeton 1977.

Crone, Patricia. *The Nativist Prophets of Early Islamic Iran*, (Reprint) Cambridge 2014.

Curtis, Vesta Sarkhosh and Stewart, Sarah (eds). *Birth of the Persian Empire (The Idea of Iran vol 1)*, London 2005.

Curtis, Vesta Sarkhosh and Stewart, Sarah (eds). *The Age of the Parthians (The Idea of Iran vol 2)*, London 2007.

Curzon, Lord G. N. *Persia and the Persian Question*, London 1966.

Darbandi, Afkham and Davis, Dick (ed and trans). *Farid ud-Din Attar; The Conference of the Birds*, London 1984.

Daryaee, Touraj. *Sasanian Persia: The Rise and fall of an Empire* London 2007.

Daryaee, Touraj. *Sahrestaniha-i Iranshahr*, Costa Mesa 2002.

Ebtekar, Massoumeh. *Takeover in Tehran: The Inside Story of the 1979 US Embassy Capture*, Vancouver 2000.

Ehteshami, Anoushiravan. *After Khomeini: The Iranian Second Republic*, London 1995.

Ehteshami, Anoushiravan. *Iran and the Rise of Its Neoconservatives: The Politics of Iran's Silent Revolution*, London 2007.

Esfahani, Hadi Salehi and Pesaran, M. Hashem. "The Iranian Economy in the Twentieth Century: A Global Perspective," *Iranian Studies*, vol. 42, no. 2, 2009, 177–211.

Farhadpour, Morad and Mehrgan, Omid. "The People Reloaded" in *The People Reloaded: The Green Movement and the Struggle for Iran's Future*, ed. Nader Hahemi and Danny Postel, Brooklyn 2010, 130–136.

Farhi, Farideh. "The Antimonies of Iran's War Generation" in *Iran, Iraq and the Legacies of War*, ed. Lawrence Potter and Gary Sick, New York 2004, 101–120.

Farzaneh, Mateo Mohammad. *The Iranian Constitutional Revolution and the Clerical Leadership of Khurasani*, Syracuse 2015.

Fenton, Tom. "The Day They Buried the Ayatollah" in *Iranian Studies* vol. 41, no. 2, April 2008, 241–246.

Floor, Willem. "The Revolutionary Character of the Iranian Ulama: Wishful Thinking or Reality?" in *International Journal of Middle East Studies*, vol. 12, no. 4, December 1980, 501–524.

Floor, Willem. *The Economy of Safavid Persia*, Wiesbaden 2000.

Floor, Willem. *Safavid Government Institutions*, Costa Mesa 2001.

Floor, Willem. *Sexual Relations in Iran*, Costa Mesa 2008.

Foltz, Richard C. *Spirituality in the Land of the Noble*, Oxford 2004.

Frye, Richard N. *Iran*, London 1954.

Frye, Richard N. *The Heritage of Persia*, London 1962.

Frye, Richard N. *The Golden Age of Persia*, London 1975.

Garthwaite, Gene. *The Persians*, Oxford 2005.

Gasiorowski, Mark and Byrne, Malcolm (eds). *Mohammad Mosaddeq and the 1953 Coup in Iran*, Syracuse 2004.

Gellner, E. "Tribalism and the State in the Middle East" in *Tribes and State Formation in the Middle East*, ed. J. Kostiner and P. S. Khoury, London 1991, 109–126.

Gheissari, Ali. *Iranian Intellectuals in the 20th Century*, Austin 1998.

Gibson, Bryan. *Sold Out? US Foreign Policy, Iraq, the Kurds, and the Cold War*, London 2015.

Halliday, Fred. " 'Orientalism' and its Critics" in *British Journal of Middle Eastern Studies* vol. 20, no. 2, 1993, 145–163.

Hashemi-Rafsanjani, Ali Akbar. *Karnameh va Khaterat (Report and Memoir)*; 1360–1363 (1981–1985) (4 vols.) and 1367 (1988–1989) (published Tehran 1999–2011).

Herrmann, Georgina. *The Iranian Revival*, Oxford 1977.

Hiro, Dilip. *The Longest War: The Iran-Iraq Military Conflict*, London 1990.

Hooglund, Eric J. *Land and Revolution in Iran 1960–1980*, Austin 1982.

Issawi, Charles. *The Economic History of Iran, 1800–1914*, Chicago 1971.

Ja'farian, Rasul. *Din va Siyasat dar Dawrah-ye Safavi*, Qom 1991.

Kamrava, Mehran. *Iran's Intellectual Revolution*, Cambridge 2008.

Kasravi, Ahmad (trans Evan Siegel). *History of the Iranian Constitutional Revolution*, Costa Mesa 2006.

Katouzian, Homa. *Sadeq Hedayat: The Life and Legend of an Iranian Writer,* London 2002.

Kapuscinski, Ryszard. *Shah of Shahs,* London 2006.

Keddie, Nikki. "The Iranian Power Structure and Social Change 1800–1969: An Overview" in *International Journal of Middle East Studies* vol. 2, no. 1, January 1971, 3–20.

Keddie Nikki R. *Qajar Iran and the Rise of Reza Khan 1796–1925,* Costa Mesa 1999.

Keddie, Nikki. *Modern Iran: Roots and Results of Revolution,* Yale 2006.

Keddie, Nikki. *Women in the Middle East: Past and Present,* Princeton 2006.

Kennedy, Hugh. *The Court of the Caliphs,* London 2005.

Ibn Khaldun (trans Franz Rosenthal). *The Muqaddimah,* London 1967.

Khanbaghi, Aptin. *The Fire, the Star and the Cross,* London 2006.

Khanlari, P Natil (ed). *Divan-e Hafez,* Tehran 1980.

Kian-Thiébaut, Azadeh. "From Motherhood to Equal Rights Advocates: The Weakening of the Patriarchal Order" in *Iranian Studies,* vol. 38, no. 1, March 2005, 45–66.

Kian-Thiébaut, Azadeh. "Women's Movement in Post-Revolutionary Iran" in *Iran Today: Twenty-five Years After the Islamic Revolution,* ed. M Hamid Ansari, New Delhi 2005, 314–329.

Kurzman, Charles. *The Unthinkable Revolution in Iran,* Harvard 2005.

Kurzman, Charles. "A Feminist Generation in Iran?" *Iranian Studies,* vol. 41, no. 3, June 2008, 297–321.

Lambton, Ann K. S. "The Tribal Resurgence and the Decline of the Bureaucracy in the Eighteenth Century" in *Studies in 18th Century Islamic History,* ed. Thomas Naff and Roger Owen, Carbondale and Edwardsville, 1977 108–129.

Lambton, Ann K. S. *Landlord and Peasant in Persia,* London 1991.

Levy, Habib (ed H Ebrami). *Comprehensive History of the Jews of Iran,* Costa Mesa 1999.

Lewisohn, Leonard (ed). *The Heritage of Sufism,* Oxford 1999 (especially his overview at the beginning of vol. 2—"Iranian Islam and Persianate Sufism," 11–43).

Limbert, John W. *Iran: At War with History*, Boulder 1987.

Lockhart, Laurence. *The Fall of the Safavi Dynasty and the Afghan Occupation of Persia*, Cambridge 1958.

Louër, Laurence. *Transnational Shi'a Politics: Religious and Political Networks in the Gulf*, London 2008.

Majd, Hooman. *The Ayatollah Begs to Differ: The Paradox of Modern Iran*, London 2009.

Majd, Hooman. *The Ayatollahs' Democracy*, New York 2010.

Malcolm, Sir John. *History of Persia*, London 1829.

Mallory, J. P. *In Search of the Indo-Europeans*, London 1991.

Manz, Beatrice. *The Rise and Rule of Tamerlane*, Cambridge 1989.

Marshall, G. S. Hodgson. *The Venture of Islam*, Chicago 1974.

Matthee, Rudi. "Unwalled Cities and Restless Nomads: Firearms and Artillery in Safavid Iran" in *Safavid Persia: The History and Politics of an Islamic Society*, ed. Charles Melville, London 1996, 389–416.

Matthee, Rudi. *The Politics of Trade in Safavid Iran*, Cambridge 1999.

Matthee, Rudi. "Education in the Reza Shah Period" in *The Making of Modern Iran*, ed. S Cronin, London 2003, 128–151.

Matthee, Rudi. *The Pursuit of Pleasure: Drugs and Stimulants in Iranian History 1500–1900*, Princeton 2005.

McDowall, David. *A Modern History of the Kurds* (Revised Edition), London 2010.

Melville, Charles (ed). *Safavid Persia: The History and Politics of an Islamic Society*, Cambridge 1993.

Menashri, David. *Post-Revolutionary Politics in Iran: Religion, Society and Power*, London 2001.

Michaelsen, Marcus. *Election Fallout: Iran's Exiled Journalists and Their Struggle for Democratic Change*, Berlin 2011.

Milani, Abbas. *The Persian Sphinx: Amir Abbas Hoveyda and the Riddle of the Iranian Revolution*, London 2009.

Milani, Abbas. *The Shah*, New York 2011.

Milani, Mohsen. *The Making of Iran's Islamic Revolution*, Boulder 1988.

Minorsky, V (ed and trans). *Tadhkirat al-Muluk: A Manual of Safavid Administration*, London 1943.

Mir-Hosseini, Ziba. "Women, Marriage and the Law in Post-Revolutionary Iran" in *Women in the Middle East: Perceptions,*

Realities and Struggles for Liberation, ed. Haleh Afshar,
   Basingstoke 1993, 59–84.

Mir-Hosseini, Ziba and Tapper, Richard. *Islam and Democracy in
   Iran: Eshkevari and the Quest for Reform*, London 2008.

Moin, Baqer. *Khomeini: Life of the Ayatollah*, London 1999.

Mojaddedi, Jawid (ed and trans). *Jalal al-Din Rumi/The Masnavi*,
   Oxford 2004.

Momen, Moojan. *An Introduction to Shi'i Islam*, Yale 1985.

Montazeri, Hosein Ali. *Khaterat-e Ayatollah Montazeri*, Sweden,
   France, and Germany 2001.

Morgan, David. *Medieval Persia 1040–1797*, London 1988.

Morgan, David. *The Mongols*, Oxford 1990.

Moslem, Mehdi. *Factional Politics in Post-Khomeini Iran*, Syracuse 2002.

Mottahedeh, Roy. *The Mantle of the Prophet*, Harmondsworth 1987.

Naficy, Hamid. *A Social History of Iranian Cinema* (4 vols.),
   Durham 2011.

Nafisi, Azar. *Reading Lolita in Tehran*, New York 2003.

Naji, Kasra. *Ahmadinejad: The Secret History of Iran's Radical Leader*,
   London 2008.

Najmabadi, Afsaneh. *The Story of the Daughters of Quchan: Gender
   and National Memory in Iranian History*, Syracuse 1998.

Najmabadi, Afsaneh. *Women with Mustaches and Men without Beards*,
   California 2005.

Navai, Ramita. *City of Lies*, London 2015.

Newman, Andrew J. *Safavid Iran: Rebirth of a Persian Empire*,
   London 2006.

O'Ballance, Edgar. *The Gulf War*, London 1988.

Olmstead, A. T. *History of the Persian Empire*, Chicago 1948.

Ostovar, Afshon. *Vanguard of the Imam: Religion, Politics, and Iran's
   Revolutionary Guards*, New York 2016.

Pahlavi, Mohammad Reza Shah, *Mission for My Country*, London
   1974 (first published 1961).

Parsa, Misagh. *Social Origins of the Iranian Revolution*, New
   Brunswick and London 1989.

Parsi, Trita. *Treacherous Alliance: The Secret Dealings of Israel, Iran and
   the US*, Yale 2007 (large print paperback edition).

Parsons, Anthony. *The Pride and the Fall: Iran 1974–1979*, London 1984.

Perry, J. R. *Karim Khan Zand*, Chicago 1979.

Potter, Lawrence and Sick, Gary (eds). *Iran, Iraq and the Legacies of War*, New York 2004.

Poudeh, Reza J. and Shirvani, M. Reza. "Issues and Paradoxes in the Development of Iranian National Cinema: An Overview" in *Iranian Studies*, vol. 41, no. 3, June 2008, 323–341.

Rahnema, Ali. *An Islamic Utopian: A Political Biography of Ali Shari'ati*, London 2000.

Ramazani, R. K. *Revolutionary Iran: Challenge and Response in the Middle East*, Baltimore 1988.

Razoux, Pierre (trans Nicholas Elliott). *The Iran-Iraq War*, Harvard 2015.

Renfrew, Colin. *Archaeology and Language: The Puzzle of Indo-European Origins*, Cambridge 1990.

Rizvi, Sajjad H. *Mulla Sadra Shirazi: His Life and Works and the Sources for Safavid Philosophy*, Oxford 2007.

Robertson, Geoffrey. *The Massacre of Political Prisoners in Iran, 1988: Report of an Inquiry Conducted by Geoffrey Robertson, QC*, Abdorrahman Boroumand Foundation, 2009 (available online at http://www.iranrights.org/english/attachments/doc_1115.pdf) (accessed 28-5-2011).

Rundle, Christopher. "Iran: Continuity and Change since the Revolution" in *Politics and International Relations in the Middle East: Continuity and Change*, ed. M Jane Davis, Aldershot 1995, 105–111.

Ryan, Paul B. *The Iranian Rescue Mission: Why It Failed*, Annapolis 1988.

Saberi, Reza. *A Thousand Years of Persian Rubaiyat*, Bethesda 2000.

Sanasarian, Eliz. *Religious Minorities in Iran*, Cambridge 2000.

Satrapi, Marjane. *Persepolis: The Story of a Childhood*, London 2003.

Savory, Roger. *Iran under the Safavids*, Cambridge 1980.

Schimmel, Annemarie. *Mystical Dimensions of Islam*, Carolina 1975.

Schirazi, Asghar. *The Constitution of Iran: Politics and the State in the Islamic Republic*, London 1997.

Shah, Idries. *The Sufis*, London 1964.

Sick, Gary. *All Fall Down: America's Fateful Encounter with Iran*, London 1985.

Sick, Gary. "Trial by Error: Reflections on the Iran-Iraq War" in *Middle East Journal*, vol. 43, no. 2, Spring 1989, 230–245.

Sick, Gary. *October Surprise: America's Hostages in Iran and the Election of Ronald Reagan*, London 1991.

Simpson, John and Schubart, Tira. *Lifting the Veil: Life in Revolutionary Iran*, London 1995.

Slavin, Barbara. *Bitter Friends, Bosom Enemies: Iran, the US and the Twisted Path to Confrontation*, New York 2007.

Spuler, Bertold. *The Age of the Caliphs*, Princeton 1999 (first ed. 1969).

Sprachman, Paul. *Language and Culture in Persian*, Santa Ana 2002.

Sternfeld, Lior. "The Revolution's Forgotten Sons and Daughters: The Jewish Community in Tehran during the 1979 Revolution" in *Iranian Studies*, vol. 47, no. 6, November 2014, 857–869.

Subrahmanyam, S. "Un Grand Derangement: Dreaming an Indo-Persian Empire in South Asia, 1740–1800" in *Journal of Early Modern History*, vol. IV, Leiden 2000.

Sullivan, William H. *Mission to Iran*, New York 1981.

Tapper, Richard. *Frontier Nomads of Iran*, Cambridge 1997.

Tapper, Richard (ed). *The New Iranian Cinema: Politics, Representation and Identity*, London 2002.

Tucker, Ernest S. *Nadir Shah's Quest for Legitimacy in Post-Safavid Iran*, Florida 2006.

Vaziri, Mostafa. *Iran as Imagined Nation: The Construction of National Identity*, New York 1993.

Wells, Tim. *444 Days: The Hostages Remember*, San Diego 1985.

Wickens, G. M. (trans). *The Bustan of Sa'di*, Leiden 1974.

Wiesehofer, Josef. *Ancient Persia*, London 2006.

Wright, Denis, *The English among the Persians*, London 1977.

Yarshater, Ehsan. "The Persian Presence in the Islamic World" in *The Persian Presence in the Islamic World*, ed. R. G. Hovannasian and G. Sabagh, Cambridge 1998, 4–125.

Zaccara, Luciano. "The 2009 Iranian Presidential Elections in Comparative Perspective" in *Iran and the International System*, ed. A. Ehteshami and R. Molavi, Abingdon 2012, 192–206.

Zibakalam, Sadegh. *Ma Chegoneh Ma Shodim*, Tehran 1999.

Zibakalam, Sadegh. "Islam, Religious Fundamentalism and Reform: A Look at the Islamic Revolution after a Quarter of a Century" in *Iran Today: Twenty-five Years after the Islamic Revolution*, ed. M Hamid Ansari, New Delhi 2005, 182–194.

Zirinsky, Michael P. "Imperial Power and Dictatorship: Britain and the Rise of Reza Shah, 1921–1926" in *International Journal of Middle East Studies*, vol. 24, no. 4, November 1992, 639–663.

INDEX